Brothers in Blood

The True Story of Ed and Alonzo Maxwell

WRITTEN BY

LES KRUGER

EDITED BY

NORA GOULD

Brothers in Blood
The True Story of Ed and Alonzo Maxwell

Published by Wheatmark™
610 East Delano Street, Suite 104
Tucson, Arizona 85705 U.S.A.
www.wheatmark.com

International Standard Book Number: 978-1-58736-996-4
Library of Congress Control Number: 2007939843

CONTENTS

Preface...5

Foreword 11

Background...13

Escape and Capture...27

Hersey 44

The Coleman Murders..65

The Coleman Funerals..74

The Coleman Inquests 80

The War and Charlie Coleman 87

Pursuit of the Maxwells.. 105

The Kentucky Story 130

Buffalo Charley 134

John Lammy and the Battle of Fox Creek 139

John Lammy's Funeral... 148

Continued Pursuit of the Maxwells... 154

The Nebraska Capture 158

Mistaken Identities 168

The Durand Lynching 174

Sensational St. Paul Journalist 187

The Durand Jail.. 195

Maxwell Editorials... 198

The Mystery of Alonzo 204

Their Final Chapters 209

Other Dates in U.S. History 219

Acknowledgements 221

Bibliography 223

PREFACE

SOMEHOW THE EPIC OF the Maxwells got lost in history. It should have been one of the biggest stories of its day because of its clandestine events: the murders of three sheriffs, the shootings of several deputies, the largest manhunt in Wisconsin history, daring burglaries and thefts linked over eight states, large bounties for their capture. All this culminating with a Nebraska shootout and a courthouse lynching by an angry crowd on an otherwise quiet afternoon. Throughout most of the Maxwells' activities, the public couldn't get enough news of their doings. Newspapers were kept busy as people clamored for more information.

So why wasn't this story as "big" as that of other gunmen who were not even as "bad"? Timing! Just when it seemed that everyone would turn their attention to these notorious desperados, Charles Guiteau shot President James Garfield in an assassination attempt. The newspapers carried little else for the next few weeks on their front pages. Other news was relegated to the inside of the papers. Every possible angle of information about Garfield and Guiteau was covered from medical updates to educational backgrounds. One article even went so far as to concentrate on the clothing the president was wearing that fateful day. His shooting occurred on July 2, 1881, just a week before the Maxwells committed their first two murders. Over the next several weeks this was the most prominently featured event in every newspaper across the country from the large city dailies to the smallest village weeklies.

Garfield died September 19, 1881. That was six days before the Maxwells were involved in another wild melee in Illinois killing a third sheriff. By the 25th, when Sheriff John Lammy lay in a creek bed with his brains blown out, the newspapers were still consumed with Garfield's death, his autopsy and his funeral scheduled for the following day. Lammy was shot on a Sunday. On the next business day the death of the sheriff was overshadowed by the coverage of the president's funeral. And the Maxwells once again escaped the wider public ridicule and disdain they so amply deserved.

The story of the Maxwells is one which needs telling. It's a story that touches on at least eight states. There is no intent to present them as romantic characters; they were merely a pair of desperados who chose to live outside the law. They do not deserve to be glorified. The people they killed were far better men than they were. Nevertheless, they are a footnote in history, so the story merits being told in its entirety as accurately as possible. That's the one element in their tale that has been missed all these years, accuracy.

Because of the duplicity of their names, to my knowledge, this work is the first time all the facts have been collected in one volume. In the state of Illinois they were known by their real name, Maxwell. In Wisconsin they lived under the alias, Williams. This too, created a situation that kept them out of the public eye. This work brings together as much information as I gleaned from Illinois where they began their notoriety, and from Wisconsin where they created for themselves a second identity. Putting the whole picture together from all the smaller puzzle pieces was a true challenge. Since they kept moving back and forth between Illinois and Wisconsin, the tough part of the assignment was keeping track of the sequencing.

The Maxwells were bad boys. Most often when one thinks of the 1880's bad guys, names come to mind like Jesse James, Billy the Kid, the Daltons, Cole and Bob Younger, John Wesley Hardin and so many others. Whether or not those outlaws really had notches on their six-shooters, they could have had because they earned them.

Just how many men they killed can be counted in some cases, in others the number is a crap-shoot. They held up trains, banks, stage-coaches and express stations. They rustled cattle, stole horses and embezzled from the Indians. Interestingly, many of them have indeed become folk-heroes.

In many ways the Maxwells equalled or surpassed the unsavoury "accomplishments" of the better known outlaws. With only limited exceptions, these rogues wholly supported themselves from their criminal activities. Expert burglars, they were also difficult fugitives to catch. And while I cannot offer them anything but scorn for their deeds, they are the only outlaws I'm aware of that murdered as many as three sheriffs and wounded other deputies while resisting arrest. These are not admirable accomplishments. These despicable statistics serve only to reinforce the heinous nature of their crimes.

I wanted to reveal the principal and peripheral characters as real people. Other than the Maxwells, most were plain folks called upon to respond to criminal occurrences in their respective towns. They were real people involved in real life at the time. To show them as they lived back then is an important piece of this book. Many were officers of the law who strove to balance maintaining safety in their towns with providing a decent living for their families. Poorly paid, they looked for the sizeable rewards offered as bounties for the likes of the Maxwells.

In many cases the people of the era had a direct link to the Civil War which was fought barely 15 years before. Many of the men had been involved in that clash and they came away from it with some definite attitudes towards what was right or wrong. It's impossible to imagine just what that war did to the way the average person viewed events for the next few years. Killings and shootings impacted far less than we might expect. The Civil War affected the degree to which people were willing to follow their sense of justice. That often meant pursuing fugitives to bring them before the law. Sometimes it even meant lynching the bad guys.

This record of the past should remind us of a time in our history when our social values and our mores were much different; of a time when people left their personal cards at others' houses, when ladies travelled with letters of introduction, when folks relied on each other as neighbours and friends, when a wayfarer could ask at a stranger's house for a meal and expect to be fed with warm hospitality rather than be turned away with suspicion and fear.

Transportation was so radically different in the 1880's: stagecoach, steamboat, horse and buggy, skiff, steam train, paddle-wheeler, horseback, ox-cart, river ferry, wagon, and even, if you can believe it, walking, sometimes for very long distances. Communication was much slower. Post could take weeks depending on the distance the note was to travel. Telegraph was quicker, but depended on whether a receiver was located at the town you wanted to reach. Whether it was or wasn't, the telegram would still have to be delivered by hand, or rather, by foot.

Photography was far from perfect. Although pictures from the era have survived by the thousands, many people never had their photo taken. The process was rather lengthy and expensive. Not every community had a photographer. Cameras were a commercial commodity and certainly weren't found in many households. Few people even knew how to operate one of those gadgets. To have a photo taken two or three times during one's life was a rarity. Fortunate was the person who ever had one picture taken. Stillwater Prison had no recorded mug-shots of its inmates until after 1890. Joliet prison took a few before that, but most apparently did not survive because storage conditions were simply not adequate to preserve the integrity of the material bearing the photo. To this day neither prison has been able to locate any mug-shots of the Maxwells. Photos had been taken, but none have survived.

Nothing in this book is fiction. It was real. The only dialogue used was all taken verbatim from the reports of the day. Nothing was added. There are no incidents or facts offered that are not recorded as having actually happened. The Maxwells were real; the things they did were real. The rest of the people in this book were as real in their time as you or I are now. They lived in a different era and it's that time period and their involvement that the story of the

Maxwells is truly about. Ed and Lon were not heroic characters. They were merely blights on the social landscape. Nevertheless, they wrote for themselves a scene on History's stage and that is what I've presented.

FOREWORD

....

"Unwritten history becomes, in the course of time, mere legend or tradition. Written history preserves the deeds of men and the events of their day, and passes them down to posterity as cherished realities or monitory guides to the paths of duty and honor.

The history here given has been for the most part, obtained from those who have been either eye witness to, or actors in the events narrated. It is well to consider for a moment the fact that time is not far distant when our actions, and the events of our time, will be commented on and read by others with an interest as great if not greater than that with which we regard those who have preceded us, and if their faults and weaknesses serve to guard us against ours, and their nobleness and self-denial integrally serve to inspire us with a spirit of emulation to duty and to right, then our history has served its purpose."

Opening statement of *Calhoun County – Its Early History and First Settlers* created to celebrate July 4, 1876 celebration of the 100th anniversary of the signing of the Declaration of Independence.

Written by Sheriff John Lammy, the third lawman killed by the Maxwell brothers on September 25th, 1881.

More appropriate or ironic words could not be found to open this book.

BACKGROUND

WHILE THE STORY OF the Maxwell brothers extends into eight states, it has its beginnings solidly planted in Illinois starting about 1870. That was when David D. Maxwell, the boys' father, came from Wyandotte County in Ohio to the rural farming area near Macomb in McDonough County.

Like thousands of other men during that period, David had fought in the War Between the States. He served with the Union as a corporal in Company H with the 103 Illinois Infantry. When the war was finished, he quietly returned to civilian life to farm and raise a family.

War had a way of devastating a man's life. Fighting in the field could sometimes be the easy part. It was a regimental effort and one learned to rely on others to help carry the banner and get the nasty job done as a team. But putting one's life back together after the peace treaties were signed was a singular task. Seldom was it an easy one. Not infrequently the returning soldier found himself without a job to go back to and no regiment on which to rely for support. Family, friends, lovers all had to be re-acquainted. A badly wounded soldier might have been so maimed that he may never have regained the life he once enjoyed. No matter what the rank held in the army, when the uniform was off, everyone was equal, and he was left to his own devices to put his life back together somehow.

For whatever reasons, Corporal David D. Maxwell was without a job. There's some suggestion that he had done some farming in his past, but he didn't seem to be rooted to any particular piece of farmland. He may have worked out as a hired hand on someone else's farm. By the time he reached the Macomb area, he was a homeless transient looking to settle somewhere that would afford him the opportunity to forge a living for his family. During the winter of 1869-70, with his family in tow, he approached Mr. E. Hicks asking to stay for the night. Hicks, typical of most folk who have lived and worked close to the land, welcomed the Maxwells for that night, and the next day allowed them to occupy a vacant house he had on his rural property in Hire Township. The family stayed until spring when Maxwell rented a piece of the land to farm. They remained there for the next few years as David began creating some stability in their lives.

David Maxwell was described as an honest, hard-working man.

The gravestone of Susan Maxwell in Osco Cemetery says she died in 1891 at age 57. The small inscription at the bottom of her marker says:
This body from the dust shall rise
And dwell where pleasure never dies.
Photo: L. Kruger

His wife, Susan, although quiet by nature, was equally diligent about maintaining a suitable home. A rather nondescript woman, little was known of her except that she maintained a comfortable, clean home for her family. Born in 1834, she was two years younger than her husband. At the time, they had four boys and one girl. Two more children would be born over the next four years for a total of seven. While little is known about the five youngest siblings, most of America was to come to know a great deal about Ed and Alonzo (often referred to as Lon). Ed, the oldest of the Maxwell off-spring, was born in 1853. He was about four years older than Lon (b. 1857). The only daughter, Flora, was born between Lon and George (b. 1866). The three youngest children, John (b. 1869), James (b. 1872) (who died at age seven in 1879) and Gilbert (b. 1874) were born in Illinois.

Considering some early accomplishments, there was no hint evident of the havoc which Ed and Lon would create in later years. They were both good students and were uncommonly bright. When he was about 15 years old, Lon won a Bible as a prize for committing to memory the most biblical verses in a year. There was some speculation later whether Lon was simply out to beat any opponents rather than to actually absorb any truths from the verses learned. In school Ed won a prize about the same time for penmanship. In later years Ed would put his talents with a pen to use generating some interesting letters from jail.

Growing up, they weren't much different than most boys their age. They enjoyed pranks and mischief and certainly weren't averse to getting into typical boyish trouble. However, the brothers had a way of adding a more destructive bent to their handiwork. One night while out coon hunting, they stole several chickens. They took them to a nearby school-house and roasted them. Having eaten the birds, their next stop was at a bee-stand where they not only stole all the combs of honey they could cart off, but they added insult to injury by maliciously upsetting the hives simply to destroy them. When it was discovered who was at the root of the damage, there was some discussion about arresting the boys. This marked the first, but certainly not the last time that they headed for the woods where they camped out until the incident was either patched up or forgotten.

In 1874 Ed moved on to his first blatantly criminal activities. In February of that year he stole two coats from the store in Blandinsville owned by C. W. Dines. Dines was pretty sure who was the culprit, so took a deputy with him to where Ed was employed at a nearby farm. While Maxwell was in the barn-yard, Dines entered the house, located the stolen articles and with the officer beside him to make the arrest, approached the thief carrying the evidence.

West side of Blandinsville main street late 1800's

When he saw them coming, Ed, knowing he was in serious trouble, did something that he would repeat on several more occasions as his criminal career escalated. He jumped on Dines' horse, threatened them by waving a pistol in their direction, and fled the place chasing off the officer's mount as well. Hours later, with a posse of 15 to 20 men on his trail, he once again headed for the woods. Almost every time he felt threatened, Ed would light out for the bush. He was in his element there and it was difficult, if not impossible, to flush him out.

At that time of year Crooked Creek was high and filled with ice. The posse expected that by securing the bridge, Maxwell would be boxed in, unable to get across the swollen stream. They were positive he would never cross the icy, dangerous waters of the creek. When they couldn't find him, they assumed he had doubled back on his own trail.

But a few days later, Dines' horse was found miles away to the north in Warren County. This too became a characteristic Maxwell escape; steal a mount, buggy or skiff, and then discard it when it was no longer of any use. But the discovery of the horse led to Ed's capture in Roseville. Brought back to the Macomb jail to face trial, he admitted to the posse members that he had indeed crossed Crooked Creek despite the peril of the high water. Ed was to become known for doing the unthinkable sometimes, especially if he were in danger or trying to avoid capture.

For stealing the clothes, the theft of the horse and the flight from the posse, Ed received his first jail sentence. With no prior offences, at least officially, he was given one year in Joliet Penitentiary. His prison record shows he was admitted April 2, 1874. He was discharged eleven months later having been granted 30 days off his sentence for good behavior.

His record revealed nothing else of any significance. Had he been in trouble during his incarceration, it would have been reflected on his record. Nothing of that nature was recounted. Of his habits, he was noted as using neither tobacco nor alcohol. Unlike most of the other prisoners, Ed was labeled literate because he could both read and write. His time in jail was just that, an unremarkable sentence served until his release on March 2, 1875.

Whether out of embarrassment about his son or for financial reasons, David Maxwell decided to leave the Macomb area that year while Ed was in Joliet. He took his family to Nebraska where he began farming at Osco in Kearney County. Shortly after his release, that's exactly where Ed headed. But he had no intention of staying long.

Ed went to Nebraska to find Lon. At some point he had determined that stealing from others was an easier way to make a living than working. He needed a partner for his crime team and nobody would make a better accomplice than would Lon. Eleven months in the pen had only served to whet his appetite for easy money. Possibly that was the result of exposure to others who were criminals. The fact that they had been caught and were doing time in the penitentiary was considered to be just part of the inevitable risk.

In his entire life, Ed was never one to have many close friends or associates, but he was devoted to his brother. Alonzo was the one constant in Ed's life. At the same time, Lon looked up to Ed and revered him. There's absolutely no doubt that they were unswerving in their loyalty to each other. They knew each other's moves and when they operated together, they were a team of practiced precision. Between them they had secret signals, pre-arranged manoeuvres and back-up rendezvous points. They relied primarily on stealth during their burglaries. They made sure that they had alternative plans should anything go awry. Every job they pulled was done with careful planning and preparedness.

By May of 1875 they were back to their old haunts around Macomb and McDonough County. They went on a burglary spree that terrorized the area for months. They broke into houses in and around the townships of Emmett, Hire, and Sciota. In Blandinsville several houses were burglarized, often as the residents were asleep in the home. Their actions were characterized by their daring and lack of fear. The fact that they were usually heavily armed no doubt contributed to their brazen attitudes.

Strangely though, Alonzo was not at first recognized as being Ed's brother. He was presumed to be a man named "Post". This may have been a ploy to keep Lon from the eye of the law as a criminal. If they didn't know who he was, he might be able to escape detection. Early on, as far as the folks in that part of Illinois knew, the robberies were being committed by Ed Maxwell and his partner "Post".

Their robberies were becoming profitable for them. Admittedly they were good at what they did. They stole hundreds of dollars in cash, not to mention equipment, goods and horses. In May and June of 1875, Ed and his partner "Post" were blamed for a rash of burglaries throughout McDonough County as well as a few in neighbouring Hancock, Henderson and Fulton Counties. From the farm of E. S. Smith in Sciota, two horses were stolen. These were discovered about 40 miles to the west near Hamilton in rough shape, having been ridden hard, and then turned out. Burglarized homes in that area attested that this pair of crooks had widened the radius from their home base.

Newspapers of the day mentioned many of the victims by name as well as reporting on the amounts stolen. These were good people living in a relatively small, close-knit community. If they could be victimized, there was merit in reporting it so that everyone else might become more vigilant. These folks, especially those that made a living close to the soil, did not have a great deal of money. In an age when a month's wages for putting up hay was less than $50, a theft of even $20 was very significant and damaging.

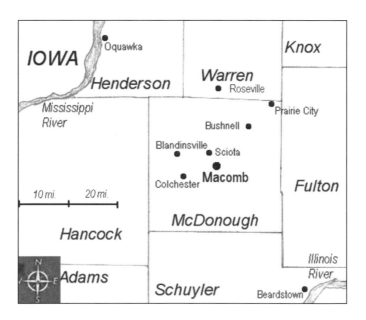

In July of that same year, the victims of the Maxwells' widening crime spree read like a census list: Mr. Ferris near Blandinsville, a small undisclosed amount of money; an unnamed person, $60; John Isom, $22 along with a pocket-book and papers; Mr. Carlisle, a pocket-book and $35 or $40 as well as a note for $900; S.B. Davis, $5 and his pocket-book; L. English, $50. Only the James Griffith family seemed to fare unscathed. They were awakened by the thieves one night and managed to frighten them off. This was certainly a rarity since the Maxwells didn't scare off easily, but they also didn't take any chances either, especially if they were unsure about the circumstances. The Griffiths could count themselves among the lucky households to have avoided being victimized by the scoundrels.

The Maxwells were rarely without a display of rifles or revolvers. It soon became their trademark. On one occasion they brazenly walked with their revolvers drawn through the small village of La Crosse which sat over the county line in Hancock County. It was almost as if they were taunting the law. The incident happened in broad daylight. The officers of La Crosse did attempt to arrest them, but the Maxwells simply outmaneuvered them. Faced with looking down the barrels of Ed's and Lon's artillery, discretion took precedence, and the officers were forced to withdraw. Later, the Maxwells leisurely left town without hurting anyone. This was the first reported incident when a lawman was threatened with Maxwells' firearms. It was to be the first of many.

There was good reason why they had no fear in such circumstances. The boys were both excellent marksmen. Often for hours at a time, Alonzo and Ed practiced both with revolvers and with rifles. With either weapon, they became expert and deadly. Ed claimed that with a Spencer rifle he could hit a door five out of every seven shots at a distance of 800 to 1000 yards, and that with a revolver he could hit a target the size of a man at 100 yards four out of five times. He was careful not to say "hit a man". But he admitted that his ability with a gun was nothing compared to the skill of his younger brother. According to Ed, Alonzo couldn't be beaten. Hours of practice had rendered him a highly proficient marksman.

The Colt Navy pistol was their favourite revolver. It was said that they preferred the Winchester rifle as a weapon of choice, but as their escapades went on, they were found to use the Henry rifle and the Spencer with equal accuracy. Perhaps it had a great deal to do with which rifle was most available or easiest to steal. But Lon was equally deadly with a buffalo gun as well, as he later demonstrated.

The Maxwells had no problem getting around the countryside. They would simply steal a couple of horses and ride them to their destinations, often as much as 75 to 80 miles in a single night, then turn loose the exhausted animals, only to swipe another pair for their return trip. This became their typical means of transportation. If horses weren't needed, they would do the same with a skiff or boat on the rivers. They were not known for kindness towards animals. Horses were nothing more to them than a form of locomotion, simple beasts of burden. They would ride an animal until it dropped, then replace it. Horses they used were frequently found "stove up" in poor physical condition, or dead. If they drove a horse pulling a buggy, they were just as reckless, often tipping or driving the vehicle to destruction.

While they showed little mercy towards animals, their disposition towards people seemed somewhat kinder. They were not known at the time for any violent tendencies towards people. All of their crimes were of a rather petty, if not aggravating, nature. Except for monetary losses and insults to one's dignity, they left no one hurt. But they were not above terrorizing their victims when confronted. Alonso McCally found that out the hard way. They stole a buggy and set of harness from McCally's barn about four miles north of Table Grove. In the morning McCally followed the buggy tracks in the gravel with the help of some neighbours.

In the Spoon River brakes, he discovered where the carriage had turned into the bush near Smithfield. His companions had previously split up, and although alone, he followed the tracks into the thicket. He came across two men with a pair of horses eating corn. As he approached the men, one of them with a gun ordered him to stop.

"What do you want?" one of the men asked.

He replied, "I want my harness; I just found my buggy over here, now I want my harness."

"Have you got a warrant?" asked the gunman in jest.

"No."

"Anybody with you?"

"No" he lied.

They invited him to come up closer and despite the revolver, McCally approached them. They returned the harness to McCally, but told him they would never be taken alive. After McCally left with his harness, he returned with a posse with every intent of arresting them. They were not to be found, but they left behind two horses and a revolver. The horses were found to belong to a farmer in Mc-Donough County from whom they'd been stolen.

On numerous occasions the Maxwells made a remark to people similar to the one they made to McCally; they would not be taken alive. Whether or not they themselves believed this, or whether the comment was only intended to generate fear in the minds of their pursuers, they mentioned it frequently enough to keep everyone on their guard. After all, it was definitely intimidating.

But the boys were wearing out their welcome in the area. Neighbours were fed up and frightened. So much so, that a group of citizens banded together to pool their finances enough to put up a reward of $500 for the arrest of the Maxwells. This was the first known occasion of a bounty on their heads. It wasn't going to be either the last or the largest.

Their antics didn't go unnoticed by the law for long. Captain Charlie C. Hays, a Civil War veteran with a record of bravery at the front, was the deputy sheriff of Schuyler County at Beardstown some 35 miles south of Macomb. Hays was only one of many law officers who had been targeting the Maxwells should they enter his jurisdiction. He had also been fairly certain that he was not looking for a Maxwell and a "Post". He said later that he had been sure that both men were Maxwells. This "gut" feeling gave Hays an advantage because, while Ed was the small man they were watching for, "Post" was described in the "Wanted" circulars as large. In fact both men were small. Ed was only five feet, three inches tall. Lon, slightly taller at about five feet, five inches was barely filling the smallish frame of his seventeen years.

Captain Charlie Hays must have learned to fight at an early age; he was the eighth of nine children. He enlisted when he was 27 with the Illinois 7ᵗʰ Cavalry serving under Generals Grant, Thomas and Sherman. For his bravery in action, he was promoted to the rank of Captain. He was captured at least once, but escaped, and he was wounded several times, never too seriously to keep him from continuing in the war.

After mustering out in November 1865, Charlie lived in Prairie City, Illinois, where he operated a grocery store before entering law enforcement. He married a second time six years after his first wife, Mattie, passed away in 1881. Charlie lived in good health well into his 80's.

Hays had been tipped off that the Maxwells were on their way down the Illinois River traveling as they often did by skiff. Looking every bit like two hunters on the river, they could easily move about without being recognized even in daylight. But this time Captain Hays knew they were coming and was prepared. On August 10ᵗʰ, 1875, he was ready for them.

Expecting them to pull in for supplies, he and two assistants were waiting near the dock. Alonzo stayed in the boat while Ed walked up to the town for supplies. The deputy sheriff and his help casually walked into the store behind him. Ed suspected nothing. Hays wasted no time. In seconds they grabbed Ed from behind, one by each arm and the other by the shoulders and threw him on the floor. Ed fought his captors fiercely, kicking and swearing, but he was plainly outnumbered. Hays, toughened by his years of army experience, was not about to tolerate any guff from somebody on his wrong side. Despite Ed's tenacity and quick movements, he was quickly and roughly subdued. They shortly had him hand-cuffed before he was able to use either of the two revolvers or the knife he was carrying. The entire arrest and accompanying fight occurred in the store out of sight of Lon who was still in the skiff at the waterfront.

Capturing Alonzo would prove to be a bit trickier. With Ed securely bound in the store, the men walked casually towards the dock where Lon waited for his brother. They struck up a conversation with him, probably river talk or fishing. Looking at the boat, they feigned an interest in buying it from him. Lon seemed agreeable and offered the men a closer inspection. After all, it was no doubt stolen anyway. They noticed that in the bottom of the boat there were two rifles. When they felt his guard was down sufficiently, they pounced on him.

But Lon was as wiry as he was dangerous and, even outnumbered, he managed to get off a wayward shot with his revolver during the fracas. Wrestling in the close confines of the skiff, Lon was no match for two larger determined lawmen despite his tenacity. Bruised and bloodied, he was quickly restrained and cuffed with his arms tightly pinioned behind him. A check afterwards revealed that besides the two rifles and the revolver in the skiff, there were also 600 cartridges and a number of rubber blankets in the boat. While escorting their second prisoner towards town, Hays told Lon that Ed was already in handcuffs and under guard. Lon's only reaction was to ask, "Did he make a row?"

Meanwhile, Ed had heard the shot down at the waterfront. Knowing his brother was under threat, he grew terribly agitated. "My God, they're killing my brother. Let me go help."

When Lon was brought into the store, the "Post" theory was instantly dispelled. The two embraced and admitted that they were brothers. "We would fight and die for each other", they said.

The capture of the Maxwells occurred at Beardstown. They were to face charges back in Blandinsville. Hays brought them as far as Bushnell that night only to discover that not all the fight had been taken out of them. Putting up at a hotel for the night with his prisoners, he had them shackled together. Nonetheless, they slipped off their boots and made an excellent escape attempt by waiting for the right opportunity to tear out of the hotel running down the street. Had they not been chained together, they might have made good the endeavour, but Captain Hays was pretty quick himself. He was described as having "pulled out after the chaps like a locomotive and caught them after a 75 yards race". They told Hays that they had agreed between them never to be taken alive. They would escape by running and, if necessary, to shoot whoever tried to capture them. Nothing in the Maxwells' book of tricks ever suggested that they surrender when their situation looked bleak.

East side of Blandinsville main street about the time Ed stole the clothing.

The next day they were taken to Blandinsville for their preliminary examination. The news traveled quickly throughout the region that the Maxwells had been caught. People were anxious to hear that they might be able to rest easier knowing these bandits were finally behind bars, that their homes and property might once again be safer. There was some street talk of mob violence taking over that would see "...the Maxwells strung up without judge or jury." These words were to become all too prophetic. But not this time. Blandinsville citizenry were content to let the law take its course.

In court the boys waived the rest of the examination which allowed them to be jailed in Macomb at the county lock-up. While there, a local reporter was permitted to visit them. He found them to be not at all like the notorious outlaws he had expected to meet. Physically they did not appear to fit the mold. At the time, Ed was 21. He was described as "considerably under medium height" and weighing about 140 pounds. He had a close-cut beard but there was nothing about his looks that would suggest "fierceness". In fact, the correspondent found Ed articulate and intelligent in his speech. This became a recurrent description of Ed. He was very capable of good manners and knew just when to be charming. Frequently he was described as "gentlemanly in deportment" and even "good-looking". Most reporters commented on his excellent physique. Although rather short, he compensated with a muscular frame that was accompanied with swift, cat-like movements. Unless completely ironed, he was always dangerous.

Alonzo was not thought to be much of a terror in his appearance either. One newsman described him as being so youthful looking, that probably "a sound spanking" would have been a more suitable punishment than prison. He was said to be "handsome" and his politeness in interacting with those whom he liked, was genuine.

But the county was reveling in the fact that both Maxwells were now in jail and that their escapades in that part of Illinois had finally come to an end.

Well almost! Like so much of the history of Ed and Alonzo, that part of their story didn't end there. It seemed as if there was always an addition to any chapter on the Maxwells.

ESCAPE and CAPTURE

LESS THAN THREE WEEKS later, while still in the county jail at Macomb, the Maxwells demonstrated once again that they were not out of business.

A daring jail-break, masterminded by Ed himself, saw him and one other prisoner make their bid for freedom. Lon was to have escaped as well and he almost made it, but during that episode, the law won.

A Macomb *Journal* reporter later asked Ed to describe the jail-break. Ed was never shy and frequently appeared to enjoy the attention lavished on him by the press. Most often, such as on this occasion, he was only too happy to detail the events. The following is from the article in the *Journal*:

> "Brother Lon and I had talked over the matter for several days; at last we let Roberts into the secret; none of the rest knew it; I was in control of the whole matter; intended to break out the night before, but there was no opportunity.
>
> The night of the break, when the Sheriff came in, I was sitting, all prepared to spring; made a remark to the Sheriff to throw him off his guard; then sprang by him. When I got outside the jail, ran north two blocks, then west a couple, and then took south; I knew where the timber was southwest of town, and struck for it.

Once out of sight of my pursuers, instead of running, I walked leisurely along, putting [my] hands in [my] pockets, whistling as [I] went out of town. Did not know if… Lon … escaped."

Lon did not escape. Sheriff Venard of Macomb, as was his usual custom, went to lock up the prisoners in their cells at 8:30. His assistant, James Blazer, opened the hall door to that area where the prisoners stay during the day. Before he was able to close it again, Ed Maxwell ran past him after roughly shoving the sheriff aside. At the same instant, Charley Roberts, the other prisoner involved in the break-out, made for the door too. Lon Maxwell was making his dash for freedom when Venard made a grab for both Maxwells.

Besides the title of Sheriff, Josephus B. Venard was also known as Captain Venard. He had served with distinction during the recent Civil War seeing service with his unit in almost every engagement in which they participated. Enlisting as a private in the 2nd Illinois cavalry in 1861, his heroics and outstanding bravery saw him rise through the ranks. He had accompanied his unit in every action they saw during the war. He mustered out as captain on January 3, 1866. Except for the five years spent in the military, most of his life was spent working on a farm. After the war, he was nominated, based on his personal popularity, for the position of Sheriff in 1874. He served only one term, but his effectiveness in that role put the Maxwells behind bars.

Dealing with three hoodlums in a jail-break was not going to slow down this veteran. He was a man of determination. As they attempted to run past him, Venard yelled to alert Blazer. Reacting instantly, he grabbed for them in an attempt to slow their progress long enough to give Blazer time to close the door. He had them in his grasp briefly, but as he grappled with them, Roberts yanked the sheriff by the hair then tried to poke Venard in the eye with his fingers. Ed managed to break loose and Roberts was right behind him. But Venard held Lon long enough for Blazer to assist, and the two managed to get the younger Maxwell back into his cell. A few days later Lon was handed a two-year sentence to be the guest of Joliet Prison.

Despite its stalwart appearance, the elder Maxwell brother managed to escape from this McDonough County jail in Macomb.

Out on the street several men had been walking near the court-house jail. One of them was the mayor of Macomb, Alexander McLean. His attention aroused by a noise over near the jail, he spotted Maxwell and Roberts as they fled the building. Almost as soon as they cleared the door, the two inmates separated. Maxwell ran up North Lafayette Street, Roberts took off on East Carroll. Realizing at once what was taking place, His Worship McLean took up the pursuit of Ed Maxwell. But Maxwell was 22 years of age and in excellent physical condition. Mayor McLean found that, at 41 years of age, his best running would be confined to the political arena.

Everyone in law enforcement in the area knew that it was Ed's habit to steal a horse to make an escape. Over the years he'd perfected a wild ride from danger on a stolen steed as part of his repertoire.

To reduce his chances this night, the local farmers were alerted by riders sent out by the sheriff to keep an eye on their stables.

Elijah Welch, a farmer north of Crooked Creek, was one of the people advised to watch his livestock. Unfortunately he didn't take seriously the warning. Less than two hours later Maxwell was recognized riding like the wind past J. B. Eakles place about five miles west of Welch's. The next morning Farmer Welch counted one less horse to feed in his herd.

It was suspected that Maxwell and Roberts might have arranged to meet in the vicinity of Colchester, about seven miles west of Macomb. Roberts, who was from Colchester, was reported to have shown up there and spoken with several people. Although the village was watched closely by the law, there was no sign of Ed Maxwell.

Postal cards were printed bearing Maxwell's description, and sent to all outlying law enforcement agencies within 50 miles of Macomb. Special telegrams were sent to newspapers in Chicago and Quincy. Every effort was made to alert the region that Ed Maxwell was loose once again and was a potential threat. It was hoped that information or tips would soon be flooding in. As an extra incentive, a reward of one hundred dollars was offered for the capture of either of the two escapees. It would be a long time before the money was paid for Ed's bounty.

Ed was always described as gentlemanly, well-spoken and articulate. Some called him good-looking and he was said to be in excellent physical condition. Almost every journalist commented on his diminutive size. At 5', 3" it was surprising that such a small man could create such a turmoil.

He managed to elude authorities for months. In fact, it was almost a year before there was anything more concrete than rumours about his whereabouts. It seemed that Maxwell had all but disappeared. But Ed was not one to stay out of trouble, so it was inevitable that eventually he would surface again.

On September 23, 1876 Sheriff Venard received the following letter from Stillwater, Minnesota dated three days before:

> Dear Sir: I wish to enquire if you want a man by the name of Ed. Maxwell, or Maxfield, about 5 feet 6 inches high, dark complexion. I have been informed -- and my information originally came from himself – that he has committed crimes in your town or county, and that there is a reward for his arrest.
>
> He is considered a desperate character in this locality. IIe has been here; he is absent at present, but he has a den near this place, and makes occasional calls. Some of his pals, while under the influence of liquor, confidently talked about his being wanted in your town or county. The last time he returned from Illinois he had lots of Elgin watches with him. Please look the matter up, and let me know if he is wanted, and how much reward, if any, there is for his arrest. Write soon as possible.
>
> I remain yours in confidence,
> MATTHEW SHORTALL
> Chief of Police, Stillwater, Minn.

Sheriff Venard wasted no time replying to Shortall's note. There was no doubt in his mind that the Stillwater lawman had very accurately described the Ed Maxwell he so desperately wanted to see again behind his iron bars. Not wasting time with the postal system, he fired off a telegram to Shortall instructing him to arrest Maxwell at the first opportunity. He assured the chief that there was an appropriate reward in place for the capture and conviction of the fugitive. Days later he received the following correspondence from Chief Shortall:

STILLWATER, MINN., Sept. 27, 1876
Venard, Sheriff of McDonough County, Ill.

Dear Sir: -- I am in receipt of yours of the 24th and judging from your letter the reward offered by the townships is conditioned that it will be paid for his arrest and conviction. I am not in possession of any evidence that would convict him, nor do I know what crime he is charged with. It has cost me some money to look the matter up, and it will cost some more to get him, besides he is a dangerous man to take, and I do not care to go any further in the matter until I am sure of the $350. Nothing less would pay me for the trouble. The reward offered by yourself is all right, and if you will be responsible for the $350 when he is arrested, I will go get him if possible. If you conclude to be responsible for the whole amount, let me know by telegraph, as he is liable to leave this part of the country.

I remain yours,
MATTHEW SHORTALL,
Chief of Police.

Venard was emphatic and terse. He quickly telegraphed to Stillwater, "Arrest him; I will be responsible."

If Chief Shortall's concern at first about the reward seemed somewhat more mercenary than professional, there were two reasons for this. Despite the dangers and uncertainty law enforcement entailed, the job did not pay well. In fact, it was often rather poor considering the long and frequently odd hours it was necessary to work. Many officers of the law found themselves having to supplement their meager salary working at other jobs for extra income. Besides, if there were expenses incurred in the process of trying to locate or apprehend a felon, they occasionally paid these out of their own pocket. Reimbursement wasn't always possible. As an incentive for perseverance on the job, any rewards for apprehending the "bad guys" could be claimed by the lawmen who made the captures.

Every officer knew that he could augment his salary by making some good arrests. Sometimes the amount was significant, as much as a full month's salary just for bringing in a single fugitive with a substantial bounty on his head. It was a good reason to focus on getting the worst of the worst off the streets and into the jails. And it was certainly a good incentive for Shortall to round up Maxwell.

The second reason for Shortall's concern with Maxwell was that the two had met on a previous occasion. For the sheriff it had been an unfortunate and embarrassing encounter. Shortall had been called to an incident involving a man firing a rifle on the Mississippi levee in Stillwater. When Shortall arrived, Ed Maxwell, the man with the rifle, got the drop on the chief and threatened to shoot him. Maxwell, as he'd shown in the past, had no fear of the law. This was not the first nor the last time he would act so brashly by threatening to shoot a law officer. Like the police in La Crosse months before, Shortall did the wisest thing under the circumstances and withdrew to seek additional assistance. But it left him with a bruised dignity as he retreated and a renewed sense of caution. It also left Shortall wondering just how big a reward it would take for him to want to face Maxwell again.

Apparently $350 was enough to convince him. In a matter of days after sending Shortall the previous telegraph, Venard was sent the reply, "We have arrested Maxwell; come after him."

The newspapers provided almost no details at the time of the arrest because the importance of the incident was its outcome. Maxwell was again ironed and behind bars. Only later were the highlights leaked out. Sheriff Shortall and Deputy Holcombe (who would eventually replace Shortall as sheriff) located Maxwell through an informant. That person was supposedly going hunting with Ed and lured him into a shed or stable near Denmark, Minnesota under the guise of securing their horses. Inside the shed with guns drawn, waited the sheriff and his deputy. Outnumbered and completely taken by surprise, Maxwell submitted without incident. Prepared at all times for a fight, he was carrying a seventeen-shot Winchester rifle and two revolvers. All three of the weapons were fully loaded.

This time it was Captain Gladden L. Farwell who made the trek
to Minnesota to pick up the prisoner. Another Civil War vet, Captain Farwell, formerly of Company D in the 28th Illinois Infantry
Regiment, was nobody to fool with. Had Maxwell entertained any
thoughts of trying to escape from this old soldier, he was wasting
good thinking time. Farwell was a man who meant business and had
little patience for miscreants like Ed Maxwell.

---

*Not all of the accounts from the Civil War were tales of hatred and hor-
ror. There were hundreds of stories of kindness and compassion found
in soldiers during the fighting. Captain Gladden Farwell's story was one
of them. A sad pall fell over his hometown of Macomb the day news arrived that Farwell had been badly wounded in an attack by the Confederates and left for dead. The incident occurred near Jackson, Mississippi.
His own regiment had determined he was killed in action and during
their retreat, he was left where he fell. When the Rebels later discovered
the officer was still alive, they sent him on to his own side to be treated
by the Union doctors. No doubt this act of kindness saved his life. After
the war he again served in the post he had left in 1861 as treasurer of
Macomb.*

If Ed were considering another escape attempt from the Macomb jail in the coming weeks, one more surprise was in store for
him on his return to that city. Officer Farwell arrived with his prisoner in tow on Saturday, October 7th. It was the last day of court
sessions. Witnesses for the prosecution had been summoned already
so that they could be on hand. If Maxwell arrived in time, his trial
would be that day. He did. It was.

The train was an hour late causing some to worry that Maxwell
had yet again managed to create a diversion. The number of people
waiting to catch a glimpse of the infamous bandit began to swell as
the minutes dragged on. By the time the train pulled into the Macomb station, a throng of more than 500 were waiting at the depot.
Disembarking amid the steam and cinders from the train, Maxwell
looked around the faces in the waiting crowd. Instead of making

him feel important, the presence of so many had an opposite effect on Maxwell. He began to feel intimidated and fearful. He knew these were not friends who had gathered on the platform.

He maintained closeness to his guards and appeared almost relieved when finally he was in the courtroom. His case was brought to the bench fairly soon. He was arraigned and wasted no time pleading guilty to the charges against him. Less than two hours after departing the train, Ed Maxwell was sentenced to two years on each of three counts of burglary against him. In all, he received a sentence of six years in Joliet Prison. After sentencing, he was immediately led away to jail.

As he had on the previous occasion a year ago, Ed consented to an interview with the reporter from the *Macomb Journal*. The journalist recorded that not only was Maxwell willing to talk, he even appeared "anxious" to discuss his affairs.

He was asked about his daring jail escape of the year before. He said that after making it through Macomb out into the countryside, he traveled about 25 miles that night. No doubt much of it was on the horse he stole from Elijah Welch. By the next night he made it to the Mississippi River which he crossed by clinging to a log as he swam his way to the Iowa shore. He wouldn't admit where he got a change of clothing, but went on to say that the following day he hopped a freight train passing himself off as a brakeman. In this disguise, eventually he managed to make it to friends in Iowa.

"I tell you, I am not viciously inclined," he stated, "but saw there was no hope for me to reform in this county. I knew I would be hunted down, so concluded to leave the state for good. I wanted to be honest."

Maxwell had a way of saying what he knew people wanted to hear and he could do it with the utmost sincerity. If he used the journalist on this occasion to carry a pathetic message of sympathy about himself, it was not to be his last attempt. Self-serving pathos was Ed's specialty. He went on to say, "Had what may seem to you a queer notion – wanted to follow my business until I got money enough to buy a little farm of 40 or 80 acres, then marry, settle down, and live an honest life This was my intention and pride."

Maxwell continued to describe his flight from justice. After Iowa, he went on to Minnesota where he often passed himself off as a hunter. Most of the time he remained in rural areas where he was never too far from the woods which could provide him with cover should he need it quickly.

".. all last winter I went to a country district school," he added. "I behaved myself, acted honorably and learned." Revealing a softer side than had been before known of him, he claimed to have fallen in love with a country girl. He said that he had "prayed earnestly for strength" to keep him on the straight and narrow. The reporter added that at that juncture of their conversation, Ed managed to become slightly mournful, actually shedding tears. It might be useful to point out that on no other occasion in the remainder of Ed's years, was there ever a reference by him or anyone else to a damsel in his life. Had the lady been anything more than a convenient figment for this interview, it cannot be determined. Nevertheless, this seemed to be the sole reference to any amorous affection in Ed Maxwell's life.

Inquisitive about how Maxwell came to be arrested in Stillwater after such an extended period of freedom, the reporter questioned him on the events of the recent days. "I had been at a party that day … About sundown a man I knew came and asked me to go hunting wild geese on the lake, three miles away; went (by) horse-back. When there, this man took my gun and told me to go in the stable and tie my horse. While there I was pounced upon by the authorities, and arrested before I was aware I had been given away."

It was obvious that meeting Ed in person had an impact on the reporter. He described Ed as a "nice appearing, pleasant spoken little fellow". Neither a smoker nor a drinker, Ed was estimated by the journalist to weigh about 140 pounds. He said Ed had "manly and winning ways". These were characteristics mentioned repeatedly by other journalists later. Both Maxwell boys had personalities that were likeable and endearing to those who were allowed to get close to them.

In a last-ditch effort to win over the citizens of McDonough County, Ed asked the newspaperman to tell everyone that it was his intention to behave himself while in prison and to be assured that after his release, he would live an honest life.

Ed Maxwell, now Prisoner number 242, was received at Joliet on October 9th 1876. There he had his height taken (5 feet 3 inches) and his eyes and hair recorded as both being dark brown while his complexion was noted as dark. He was officially registered as having no particular religion and his occupation was given as "shoemaker". Just where or when he learned that skill remains a mystery, but later, during his sentence, both he and Lon worked in the boot shop. True to his words to the journalist, Ed did behave himself in prison. Whether it was because he recalled an early release for good behavior during his previous stay at the Joliet facility, or whether he simply avoided any disruptive habits, his prison record does not reveal any blemish during the six years he remained there as guest of the State of Illinois.

Illinois State Penetentiary for Men—Jolliet circa 1900.
Photo by F. W. Hanley

Or perhaps it was because he entertained another idea for securing an early release. Unlike many of his fellow inmates, Ed could both read and write. With a great deal of time at his disposal, he resorted to a letter-writing campaign aimed at securing for himself both the forgiveness of his victims and possibly a pardon for his crimes.

His letters were not all addressed directly to the newspaper. Several were sent to acquaintances, but with the obvious desire the contents would reach the audience he sought. And he had a way of saying what he thought his readers would want to hear. A letter to John Isom was a good example.

Isom, a resident of Blandinsville, was one of many people owning homes that the Maxwells had invaded and robbed. His house was victimized during the raids of July 1875 as was the domicile of the Mr. Carlisle he mentions towards the end of the letter. Since that time, Isom had befriended Maxwell and tried to steer him on the lawful path of the straight and narrow. A God-fearing man himself, he had given Maxwell a gift of a Bible with the hope that being drawn closer to God might draw Ed further from his outlaw ways. Knowing that Isom would appreciate hearing he was putting the Good Book to good use, Maxwell made frequent references in his missive to having read the Bible and repenting of his crimes. It was always Ed's habit of saying what he thought people wanted to hear.

Isom's background was replete with personal tragedies. He had lost both parents to smallpox within ten days of each other and was forced to live at an early age with a neighbouring family. Captured at the Battle of Chickamauga, he had become a prisoner of the rebels during the Civil War and was housed in some of the worst hell-holes the confederates called prisons, including Andersonville. Altogether he was imprisoned 528 days in the "pens of death". When he was released at the war's end, he was in terrible physical condition. He mustered out in March, 1865. After marrying, he and his wife lost two of their children in infancy and another girl at aged 15. He made his living in cattle and livestock, buying, feeding and selling them. Throughout all his misfortunes, it was John's faith in his religion that had helped him survive. Perhaps with the gift of the Bible, Isom felt that Ed too could be salvaged from his self-destructive ways.

Dated at Joliet, March 4, 1877, Ed's letter rambled through several stages all aimed at convincing folks of his reformation, begging their forgiveness and soliciting their assistance at getting his sentence reduced. In fact, he even went so far as to hint at receiving the governor's pardon.

(An interesting side-note is that the *Macomb Journal* prefaced the publication of Ed's letter with the unusual headline "Our Ed". This wasn't any reflection of good-will however, because the second line of the same heading read, "which refers to Maxwell, the Free-Booter". Obviously the editorial staff had correctly identified the not-so hidden scam behind the intent of his letter.)

Dear Friend: … hoping this will find yourself and family enjoying the best of health, and prospering, as this leaves me, the same, and most of all, a better man, with a fixed purpose to be one hereafter, and I sincerely hope, that you … and all the others who know me, will forgive me for all my cruel and unjust acts towards you and all others that I have committed, and that you will not feel too hard on me for what I have done. …

Yet, I know I have gone so far, and wronged so many, that they have utterly lost all hope and confidence in me over trying to do right hereafter. But I still hope and pray to God, that I may still have friends among you yet. And Mr. Isom, many a bitter tear, I have shed in my lonely cell for my past conduct towards my fellow men, and the distress and grief I have caused my poor mother and father, who even now do not know where I am, for I fear to tell them, for it might be the means of my losing my poor mother…… if I could recall my past conduct, willingly would I have done so long before now. But, as it is, I shall try to do better hereafter.

That Bible that you and Mr. G. W. Hainline gave me as a present, I still have, and every night, after my work is done, I read a chapter in it − not for appearances, but for my own good, and I pray to Him, the giver of all good and perfect gifts …

(Note: George Hainline was a small farmer on 60 acres outside Blandinsville. Although known to favour the Republican Party, he was also noted to be very un-political. It's unclear just how Ed might have thought Hainline could or would be of any expedient assistance in his suit.)

Ed devoted almost the entire letter to this point proclaiming his repentance. The tone of his letter was one of sincerity. He solicited the forgiveness of those he wronged and appeared to deeply feel remorse. From his daily Bible readings he said he had come to realize a deeper spiritual side of himself and begged people to give him another chance.

The next part of his note was almost laughable. He blamed his problems on falling in with bad friends, without for a minute recognizing that it was he who was the bad company.

> … I see the error of my ways. If I had not got into bad company, I would not be where I am … I fell in with bad ones and, from little to worse, have come to the penitentiary… I am in the shoe shop siding boots, and do from 13 to 14 pairs per day. My brother is lasting shoes. He is working in another shop and I cannot get to speak to him. I see him about every day at a distance. I never look at him but what I think of my past conduct, and it makes me feel very wretched indeed…

Maxwell spent considerable energy thus far in his letter to express his sorrow and regrets. But towards the latter stages of the note, he began to ease into the real reason for all this expression of remorse:

> There are a great many of us here together – about 1350 in all – and a great many of them are pardoned and quite a number have had their sentences lessened by the Governor of the State, and I often wish I hadn't acted as I did and then I might have had friends to help me too, in time of need. But I still hope you will have mercy on me for once and, Mr. Isom, if I should get my lawyer to try to get my sentence shortened, would you and Mr. Carlisle be willing to sign it to help me. I don't think I deserve a pardon, so I will not ask for one. I would like to have my time lessened so I could do

some good for myself and others, and not have to spend the best years of my life in here…I hope to hear from you soon, — My respects to you and your family.

I remain your true and sincere friend,

E. Maxwell

P.S. Please write to me soon, if you will be so kind.

It became rather clear exactly what Ed Maxwell was after. If he could convince someone on the outside, preferably with some influence, to vouch for him, he might be able to have his term reduced. Whether or not John Isom fell for Maxwell's ruse is not a matter of record. But in any event, Ed was still in prison with no sign of a reduction by early June of that same year.

Alonzo took up Ed's cause and attempted to solicit the co-operation of the good Sheriff Charlie Hays, the very man who arrested the Maxwells after capturing them at Beardstown two years before.

Using a little more diplomacy, the editor printed Lon's letter under the title, THE MAXWELLS. Below that, in smaller type ran the line: 'Interesting Letter from "Lon" to Sheriff Hays'. This letter, like Ed's was dated from Joliet Prison. It was written June 7th, 1877 and addressed directly to the lawman:

I wrote to you some two months ago, and have received no answer as yet. Thinking my letter unsent or misdirected, I again take upon myself the unwarranted liberty of writing to you, hoping that with this one I will be more fortunate. Charlie, the request I am about to ask of you is a large one to me, and perhaps I am too presumptuous in asking it, but I have no other friend to go to in that part of the country. My request is this: that you will give me your co-operation in trying to get a pardon for Ed, or a commutation of sentence.

Charlie, he is sincerely repentant of his past conduct, and declares he will lead a better life hereafter …he now sees that it would be better to settle down and live the life of a quiet, inoffensive citizen, than to be always in dread of the law and prison.

He has become convinced that what is made dishonestly never will do a person any good: he says the man is sure to lose the amount sometime in this world, let alone what is to come in the next. He has tried the wrong way, and found it a hard road to travel; he now wants to try the right.

Alonzo's letter rings remarkably like the one written a few months before by Ed. The gist of both was pretty plain. Ed was sorry and deserved to be given another chance. But beyond the content and general tone of the letter, the syntax and the sentence constructions, not to mention the over-use of commas, also are rather indicative that these two letters may have come from the same hand. Even some of the vocabulary, in words such as "hereafter", is similar. Without having access to the original handwritten papers, it would be impossible to ascertain for sure. Nevertheless there's a strong possibility that Ed wrote both letters. Certainly the philosophy and logic are identical:

> …And Charlie, when a man has done wrong and sees it, and wants to try and make amends for his conduct by trying to make himself useful to humanity, I don't think it a good policy to keep on punishing him, but give him a chance… Ed and I will live up to what we say.

Like Isom's letter sent in March, this one too was blunt in getting to the point. But now the aim was not just the possibility of a reduction of the sentence, but a blatant request for an outright pardon. And just to be on the safe side, it followed with a personal apology to Sheriff Hays for past wrongs and misdeeds:

> It's too soon to try to do anything now, but when the time comes to try for a pardon, I will have strong hopes of your having several of the most influential men of McDonough county ready to sign a pardon for him. I think if we could get his honor the Judge, and States Attorney Wheat, along with Mr. Isom, Mr. Carlysle, Mr. Pullem, and the Mayor of the city, and a few other influential men,

that they would be sufficient to influence the Executive at Springfield to grant him a pardon.....

... When I think of our poor parents and the trouble we have caused them, especially our poor old mother, I feel grateful for having our depredations nipped in the bud....

Charlie, if Ed or I have said or done anything to offend you, please excuse us, for it was unintentional on our part. – Please write to me soon and tell me without reserve whether I have been too premature in my plans.

Excuse all errors and bad writing. Ed sends his best respects, and hopes you will write soon and send us good news.

Yours truly,
Alonzo Maxwell

Whether Ed wrote both letters is an issue not easily resolved. What is certain is that Ed and Alonzo Maxwell both completed the full terms of their sentences. Alonzo was released on July 8th, 1877. Ed remained incarcerated until his release date on January 21, 1881 with no reduction of his sentence and with no pardon.

HERSEY

HERSEY, WISCONSIN WAS A small place. A very small place. It was small enough that a man could blend inconspicuously into the tiny hamlet. Located on the eastern edge of St. Croix County, it barely had village status in the early 1880's. A general store, the post office, and a scattering of houses made up the community that mostly served the outlying farms. It was an ideal place to remain anonymous from the rest of the world.

Besides the agricultural interests of the area, its one industry centered around the bountiful forests of that part of the state. Logging and the secondary businesses it spawned were prominent in the vicinity. Most of the landscape surrounding the tiny town was either farmland or forested. The prospects of a job in the lumber sector drew Alonzo Maxwell to Hersey during the fall of 1879.

Hersey today is still a very small village.
Photo: L. Kruger

Why he chose tiny Hersey is unclear. Whether he came to escape his past and start a new life, or whether he was looking for new territory in which to continue his old outlaw ways, is uncertain. What is certain is that he eventually did both. What is also vague is where he had been between his release date of July 8, 1877 from Joliet State Prison and his appearance in Wisconsin. As yet, there is no accounting for that gap in his life.

In those days Hersey, for a small place, was booming. The wood industry had lots of openings that offered a man an opportunity to make a good salary. Lon was one of many young men lured to the area by the promise of work there. For Lon, this would mean a fresh start. It was a place that offered a brighter outlook and his unsavoury past was unknown. It was a quiet town where people were more concerned with today's challenges and tomorrow's prospects rather than yesterday's troubles. He probably considered it a place where he could bury his past. He secured a job working for E.C. Austin, a lumberman well-known in Hersey.

A letter in the *Hudson Star* on August 5, 1881 signed "Edward Wolf and Brothers" may provide the most important clue why Lon selected Hersey as a place to live. In the note Ed Wolf says he had known Lon for ten years and that Lon had "boarded at my house and behaved like a gentleman all the time he was here…" It appears reasonable that Lon selected Hersey having an offer of a place to stay with the Wolfs and the prospect of work in the area.

But the Maxwell story takes an important twist with Lon's move to Hersey. In order to completely shed his past as Alonzo Maxwell, the horse thief and outlaw from Illinois, Alonzo "Williams" was born. The new surname would become the one by which Wisconsin and the surrounding area would know him, and later his brother, Ed. The adopted name may have had some significance to him at the time, or perhaps it was merely a random choosing, but there doesn't appear to be any obvious relevance to the choice of his new surname.

His first and second names were "borrowed" as well. He now called himself Lawrence David. Although David was his father's name, there's no accounting for the "Lawrence".

His brother was still serving his six-year sentence in Joliet. Meanwhile, free of Ed's influence, Alonzo (now Lawrence) found legitimate employment at a stave factory near Knapp. Working for wages was new for Lon. For almost the first time in his life he was making an honest living, settled somewhat in a community in which he made friends, and he looked forward to a period of relative ease of conscience. No longer was he continually watching over his shoulder for the long arm of the law.

His own rural background helped him to assimilate smoothly into the community. He was liked by his friends and seemed to fit nicely into the social fabric of the area. A year later, in a sworn affidavit, his step-father-in-law, William Thompson wrote that Lon "… was thought a good deal of at Hersey." His naturally pleasing personality helped him win many friends.

As well, his boyish good looks made him attractive to the ladies of the district. He was thought to be both handsome and charming. With his light brown hair and piercing blue eyes, many of the local ladies had set their sights on him.

Handsome by any standards,
Lon had a following of young ladies.

One of those infatuated young women was a pretty girl with a somewhat introverted personality. Despite being a little shy, Fannie Hussey made it clear she was interested in this good-looking lad. For his part he was enthralled with her beauty and girlish personality. Lon was not averse to acquainting himself with attractive ladies, and every account suggests that Fannie was indeed remarkably beautiful.

His fleeting engagement before marriage to Fannie has spawned several stories. One story says she met Lon at a New Year's dance in Knapp four miles away. Of course, Hersey was small enough that he had often seen her and briefly spoken with her, but they brought in the New Year together that night at Knapp. The story goes that they met that evening, danced the night away and were married the next day.

All this, of course, belies the necessity of obtaining a marriage certificate, finding a preacher willing to perform the ceremony on such short notice, and securing the blessings of the relatives. But it does make for a rather romantic anecdote, albeit somewhat far-fetched.

The true account is that they were married in Hersey on July 5, 1880 by Justice of the Peace, C.D. Field. The marriage registration reveals almost all of the information accurately except that Lon changed his parents' surnames to match his own. His first two names are reversed also for some reason, possibly a clerical error at the time. His occupation was listed as "millwright". Fannie's middle name was not recorded.

For the first months of their marriage they lived together in Hersey as Mr. and Mrs. Lawrence Williams. He was 22 years old, Fannie was 16. Exactly when he began using the name "Alonzo" again is not certain, but many of his Hersey friends were later to call him by that name.

Things were going well for the newly-weds. They had the support of her mother and step-father living close-by in the same village, and Alonzo was making a good livelihood cutting wood. Like their neighbours, they supplemented their larder with fresh vegetables from their garden and had some basic farm stock such as a cow and some chickens to provide further for their table. They weren't rich, but they were happy with the necessities life and Lon provided. The young couple was popular within the small circle of friends in the neighbourhood.

Their happiness, however, was short-lived. Lon had contracted to cut cordwood during the winter of 1880-81 for Wilson, Van Vliet and Company. While working with an axe in the bush, he cut his foot badly through his heavy leather boot. The foot soon became infected and it was necessary to amputate one of his toes. The surgery was performed by Dr. Ed Baker of Hersey who removed the toe next to the big one on his right foot. Although the incident seemed minor, its impact proved to be significant for two reasons. It was a means by which he would ever afterwards be unmistakably recognized. The final proof positive of identifying Alonzo Maxwell was to examine his right foot. This was to be done on several occasions. Later as a fugitive, it meant he had to hide this defect from prying eyes to remain anonymous. It also left him with a slight lameness although it was barely detectable to anyone who wasn't aware of the problem.

But more importantly to his story, the injury put him out of work. The timing couldn't have been worse. Fannie was now pregnant, and Lon, unable to support himself and his wife adequately, became depressed with the situation. Bills began to mount. He saw little means of getting by financially. Lon was a labourer and being physically unfit meant his days of working were limited. That left his spending-power limited too.

But fate had a way of intervening. Ed completed his prison term at Joliet. According to his convict record, he was discharged January 21, 1881. The brothers had always been close and it was reasonable that Lon kept Ed posted via letters about his new life. Judging from the timing, Ed must have traveled straight to be with Lon shortly after the iron doors of Joliet closed behind him on his release. Since he had no other close friends, he naturally gravitated to Lon knowing he could count on his brotherly support now that he was again on "the outside".

His transition to Hersey impacted negatively on Lon's relationship with Fannie. Apparently Fannie was unable to warm up to Ed. He was cut from a coarser cloth than was Lon, and no doubt his six years spent in Joliet had left him with some rather rough edges. Locked up in prison with 1500 other inmates, Ed had not improved his social skills. Fannie found him devoid of the gentler side she had discovered in Lon.

His presence in the house also commanded more attention from Alonzo. Not having any friends or acquaintances of his own, Ed stuck close to Lon most of the time. The two were constantly together as they had been in their days of youth. Much to Fannie's chagrin, this meant taking a back seat in her relationship with Lon. Most of her husband's time was now consumed with his brother. It seemed they were inseparable. With the wasted six years to catch up, the boys filled their hours in each other's company. Fannie soon found herself somewhat of an outsider. Her one salvation in this was that her mother, Bridget, and her new step-father lived within walking distance which meant she had someone with whom she could feel comfortable.

Another mouth to feed in Fannie & Lon's household had also put additional pressure on their pantry. After six years' imprisonment at

Joliet, Ed arrived in Hersey with little more than the clothes on his back and an appetite. While they had some basic staples from their barnyard for the table, it would be several months before there was going to be any truck from their garden. Flour, sugar, salt and other necessaries had to be purchased. Lon's savings were depleted and, even though his in-laws tried to help, there seldom seemed to be enough. Their financial situation was becoming critical.

Lon was beginning to become depressed and his despair showed every day as he saw the worry and unhappiness in Fannie's eyes. Her pregnancy combined with their failing economic status was rapidly having a toll on the couple. It didn't take Ed long to suggest a fast solution to this predicament. His quick-fix was for the two of them to return to the life they had so successfully carved out for themselves years before. According to Ed, if they went back to the outlawry they knew so well, their financial woes would soon be in the past.

Lon was opposed to returning to their life of crime. By now he really had intended to put all that behind him and pursue a legitimate living. After all, he was married to a sweet girl and he wanted the baby they were expecting to be brought up in a happy, secure family environment. It's not clear at this point whether Fannie even knew of Alonzo's true past. If she knew, it was likely she accepted that he had paid for his past crimes and was willing to get on with him in his improved future. If she did not know, then it was highly probable that Lon wanted to keep his past from her to protect her or prevent her from being hurt. Either way, returning to the old ways would definitely be disruptive to the life he envisioned with Fannie.

But in the end, Ed's persistence and Lon's bleak fiscal future won out. After all, they had been good at what they did. While they had never got rich, they obviously had enough money as a result of their thievery that they continued at it until they were apprehended. Horse stealing and burglaries were profitable enough that they always had sufficient funds to get along. Since neither was skilled at any particular trade, their crime sprees paid better than the menial jobs at which they would be employed had they chosen to work for a living.

At first it was a few simple farm burglaries in the immediate vicinity. Successful at these, it didn't take them long before they were back to creating a full-time career for themselves on the wrong side of the law. Most of the break-ins were not reported in the papers because they were so intermittent and scattered. If the papers gave any information at all, it was simply that the thefts had occurred at someone's place with a list of what valuables were stolen. Nobody attached any blame to the "Williams" brothers. At that stage they were an unknown quantity. Until then, there were not enough incidents for the law to establish any pattern to the crimes. Although the Maxwells were using the same routines they had perfected in Illinois, these were not yet recognized in Wisconsin. Had he been privy to the reports, McDonough County Sheriff Venard would have spotted the Maxwells' tell-tale "modus operandi" in short order. The only aspect that the boys had changed was the name of the state.

In the spring they began making small forays into the nearby countryside breaking into homes and stealing what they could easily carry off. Since these bandits hadn't been in the area long, it wasn't likely that they would be easily recognized. As they did during their ventures in the past, they added extra insurance by always traveling heavily armed. Added to their repertoire were small techniques gleaned over the years. They had learned, for example, that putting a few drops of whiskey in a horse's nostrils would keep it from whinnying while they spirited it away. Little tricks of the trade like that helped to add confidence to their brashness.

Gradually they expanded their territory into surrounding areas which meant they would be away from home "working" a little longer. Ed & Lon could go off to "work" for a couple of days at a stretch, and then return to Fannie at Hersey. Whether or not Fannie knew what they we really doing is not clear, but Lon was devoted to his wife and no doubt would have protected her from the truth. He knew her sensitivity would cause her undue stress. As their "work" took them farther afield, instead of being gone for a night or two, they were often gone for a week or two. More and more frequently Fannie languished at home alone and her loneliness left her feeling more uncomfortable and apprehensive. Her pregnancy and her own insecure demeanor contributed to her uneasiness.

The boys were back to their old pattern of stealing horses, sometimes with buggies, travelling to distant townships to commit their crimes where they were less recognizable, then returning to their home-base. It was a formula that had served them well in Illinois. Here in Wisconsin, it was almost like using a fresh approach.

It wasn't long before their activities drew the attention of the law. For the first time in that area, the Williams brothers were mentioned by name by the local newspaper. Until this occasion they had dodged any negative publicity. The May 28th, 1881 edition of the *Dunn County News* in Menonomie, Wisconsin carried the following comment:

> A couple of desperadoes named Williams, who had been living about Hersey for several months back tarried about Waubeek a couple of weeks. Under Sheriff Knight and Marshal Seely went over to arrest them when the outlaws "borrowed" Jo. Gazeley's skiff and went down the river. The last heard from [them] was that they passed Wabasha Thursday afternoon going down the Mississippi. They were heavily armed and claimed that they cannot be captured alive.

The article marked two milestones for Ed and Alonzo: it was the first time they received the attention of the newspapers in Wisconsin for their crimes, and more significantly, it was the first time the media had ever referred to them as the "Williams" Brothers. It would not be the last. In what became an ironic turnaround, as they later became more infamous for their escapades, the "Williams" brothers were said to have the alias "Maxwell". The final statement of that article was not to be overlooked either. There again was that reference that they would not be easily taken by the law. They intended to go out in a blaze of glory. Many times throughout their career, it was reported that they had sworn a pact never to be taken alive.

The spring of 1881 saw more intense activity by the Maxwell boys. By now they were taking seriously their outlawry. And they were becoming much more brazen. Sheriff Kelly of Hudson, a town on the Minnesota- Wisconsin border on the St. Croix River had a run-in with them. He traveled to Hersey with a warrant for the Maxwells' arrest for burglarizing the St. Croix Lumber Company at Baytown, taking with him the head clerk of the store, Mr. Chalmers. The Maxwells had been identified at that business the day before the break-in. Arriving at their residence, Kelly and Chalmers were met by both suspects, each brandishing two revolvers when they appeared at the door. As they had done to other lawmen in the past, they warned the sheriff to leave if he valued his life. Kelly was convinced that they might shoot him. Knowing he was not in a winning situation, the Sheriff wisely retreated to re-group and seek help for this arrest.

He had hoped to raise a posse in Hersey to help bring in these desperados, but he was in for a surprise. The people of Hersey had no desire to go against the Maxwells. They had already learned that it was far better to be a friend to them than to risk their wrath. Kelly concluded that the village was terrorized by the two men. He could not get anyone locally to move against them. Instead he returned to Hudson to raise a posse, but by the time they made it back to Hersey, the Maxwells had disappeared again.

That episode transpired in late April or early May of 1881. They were now on the lam again and once more began doing something completely unexpected. Maybe because they were comfortable in the area, or because they knew of more places there to pilfer, the Maxwells returned to burglarizing their old stomping grounds in Illinois. Neither had been there since their stint in Joliet. McDonough, Henderson, Fulton and Warren Counties in Illinois were familiar territory. They knew what places to hit for profit and they knew where they could hide. While they were in Illinois, the Wisconsin law enforcement lost track of the Maxwells. Conversely, when they were back in Wisconsin as the "Williams" brothers, the Illinois agencies couldn't locate them. Through the duplicity of the names and the great distance between their crime scenes, the boys were very slippery in the eyes of the law.

In Illinois their old habits and trademark techniques were soon recognized. Their methods weren't sophisticated or flamboyant, but they were characteristic. The *Macomb Journal* cited the Maxwells as the perpetrators of the night raids because "… the bold daring manner of the thieves is pretty conclusive proof". Things were so bad in the area around Blandinsville that neighbours in the region had banded together to form a vague little group called the Mystic Brotherhood of Justice. The objectives of this loose fraternity, according to reports it released to the press, were to suppress crime, provide home protection, aid innocent parties in obtaining justice and enforce the law against criminals. It was backed by funds which were gathered by "assessments" and in 1881 had a membership over 100. Its existence was a clear indication that the good people of McDonough County were fed up with being victimized by burglars and horse thieves such as the Maxwells. A rather unobtrusive little group, it functioned somewhere between a CrimeStoppers organization and a vigilante committee.

Courtesy University of Western Illinois

William Neece

Horse and equipment thefts had long been trademark Maxwell jobs. The theft of Mr. William Neece's buggy and harness was a classic piece of thievery by the two. It was also seen as an act of personal revenge as Neece had been the District Attorney who had prosecuted the boys in the past. Two horses had been stolen in Henderson County in Illinois. A saddle and bridle were left in Neece's barn when they stole his buggy and harness. Not an equal exchange considering the price of a comfortable carriage against that of a worn saddle. But the ploy had all the earmarks of a Maxwell job; steal a horse or two, ride them for miles, and then swap them somewhere for another or different means of transport. The *Macomb Journal* of June 23, 1881 reported the incident stating that Neece later recovered his badly damaged buggy in Fulton County, several miles away. Backtracking to the original thefts in Henderson County, Sheriff J.O. Anderson of that county received the following missive dated June 14 from the horses' owner:

> … they crossed the river (Illinois) three miles above Peoria at ten o'clock Saturday night, at the rope ferry -- on the regular horse thief trail, -- giving the ferryman a dollar to set them across: (he only charges 20 cents for a team). One of them was riding without a saddle, on a horse-blanket; had a pair of broad buggy lines… One of the men was low, heavy built, with small black moustache. The ferryman failed to describe the other man… They were also seen by a boy out hunting; they had gone through a cornfield… they presented their guns … have repeating rifles; will perhaps be bad ones to take as they also carry revolvers.

The descriptions of the men and the methods they used to steal the horses and equipment, changing some along the way, all pointed to the work of Ed and Alonzo. The fact that they were heavily armed further confirmed their identity. Repeated raids in the night kept the local officials desperate to try to catch up with them. Sheriff Anderson wrote to his wife on June 6th:

> I will write you a word or two while waiting for the train…. I enclose you a slip cut from today's *Peoria Journal* …. By reading it you will see what I have been doing. I have been going night and

day since I left home, and don't expect much rest until I catch the thieves.

Whether it was intended to alleviate any worries his wife might have had about him, in an ironic bit of understatement Sheriff Anderson concluded the letter to his wife with the following comment:

They are regular desperados, have drawn guns on several persons but I don't think they will use them.

The clipping that Anderson sent his wife was a record of how the search for the horse thieves was being handled and the progress of the crooks as they made their way through the county. The following excerpt from that article holds an interesting incident:

… The thieves with their horses crossed the river at the narrows above Peoria Saturday night … where coming to a school house they placed the (stolen) horses in a coal shed, while they went into the school house to rest.

Sunday morning a farmer living near the school saw the head of a horse in the coal house, and went over to see what was up. He found two white horses there, and going to the school house, opened the door when two guns were within a foot of his head backed up by two young men.

"Don't shoot me!" cried the frightened farmer, and (after he) left the thieves immediately took their horses and started this way.

… The thieves went to a farm house this side of Blue Town, giving up a silver watch for something to eat. They told the farmer that they were out hunting squirrels and would be back for dinner. On leaving they threw their guns over their back fastened by straps and started off.

Anderson was not the only lawman on the lookout for these crooks. In that first newspaper report in Wisconsin of the activities of the "Williams", Under-Sheriff Knight was mentioned in the Menonomie article. He was Miletus Knight, a man who was well known and highly respected in Durand, the seat of Pepin County. And he was a persistent lawman. In his jurisdiction crime was taken seriously. Together with Sheriff Peterson, he set out to find these Williams brothers who were menacing their county.

In early June Ed and Lon drove a horse and buggy a short ways into the country to the farmhouse of a Mrs. Senz. No doubt this unit was stolen in a theft similar to the one stolen from Mr. Neece in Illinois. The Maxwells rarely stole a buggy for gain, but only to use it as a means of transportation. Employing as much charm as he felt he needed on the old lady, Ed convinced her to allow them to leave their buggy and horse at her place until they were able later to reclaim their possessions. Mrs. Senz agreed to their request with their promise that she would be reimbursed on their return for the feed for their horse.

In small rural communities news travelled at the speed of young boys and old ladies. It didn't take long for news of the buggy secreted at the Senz place to pique the curiosity of Sheriff Knight. After conducting his investigation and determining it to be stolen property, Knight confiscated the horse and carriage.

By this time the Maxwells' outlawry had escalated to the point that they were almost away more than they were home. In her pregnancy Fannie was unable to maintain a place by herself. Her mother, Bridget, had married William Thompson after a suitable mourning period following the death of Fannie's father. The Thompsons had been living in Hersey, but according to Bridget, they had moved to Arkansaw, about 3 miles west of Durand on April 18th, 1881. A couple of months later, Fannie moved in to be near her mother. The loneliness of her husband being away so much left her nervous and apprehensive. For her peace of mind and companionship, she was more comfortable living with her mother and step-father. Because most of their possessions were left in Hersey, her move was intended to be only temporary.

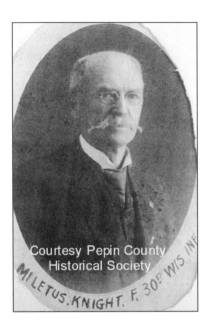

Courtesy Pepin County
Historical Society
MILETUS. KNIGHT. F. 30ᴾ WIS INF

Miletus Knight followed up the stolen goods recovery from Mrs. Senz' place. Knowing that the Maxwells (known to him by their alias, "Williams") had stolen the horse and buggy, he began his investigation with the only information at his disposal. He knew that Fannie was Lon's wife. Following up on his lead, Sheriff Knight attended at the Thompson home on an evening in early July. There he interrogated Fannie about the horse and about her husband. It's believed that by this time Fannie was fully cognizant of her husband's background, real name and his nocturnal employment. Whether or not she approved can only be a matter of conjecture. There was no indication that either her mother or step-father was knowledgeable about Ed's or Lon's habits.

Only 17 years old, Fannie was intimidated by the lawman. She was either unable or unwilling to answer his questions about Alonzo, his whereabouts or his activities. But Miletus Knight was a persistent professional. Not satisfied that she was being truthful, he pressed his point. He made it clear that he intended to capture Fannie's husband and to take him to jail to face punishment.

By the time Sheriff Knight left, Fannie's emotional state was precarious. The visit is reported to have so upset the weakened girl that within days, she went into early labor. On June 13, 1881 during the childbirth, the baby was stillborn and Fannie died. Two days later she was buried in Waubeek cemetery, a short distance north from Arkansaw on the road to Eau Galle.

During this time Lon was with Ed somewhere "working". He knew nothing of his wife's death. Fannie's mother, Bridget, had no way of notifying him.

He was not even in Wisconsin to read the death notice that appeared in the *Pepin County Courier* on June 17:

Died: — In Waubeek, June 13th 1881, Fannie Thompson, Mrs. Williams by marriage, only daughter of Mrs. William Thompson. She died at six in the evening, but in the morning of her life. Every means was used to save her life but failed. God has suffered it — it therefore must be well, and we submit with patience though it gives us pain. Funeral at the M.E. Church in Arkansaw, attended by a large circle of friends. Sermon by Elder D. Downer; text, John 14:3.

Fannie's obituary raises some curious points. It names her as Fannie Thompson. But Thompson was the name of her step-father, the man her mother Bridget married in a second relationship. There is no indication that he ever adopted her to take his surname. In fact, her tombstone names her "Fannie B. Hussey" which would have been her birth, or maiden name.

The death notice also refers to her as "Mrs. Williams by marriage". A strange wording! Had Fannie been aware of Lon's real identity? He was known in Wisconsin as Lawrence or Alonzo Williams, and it wasn't for some weeks to come before Pepin County folks would learn his true identity. By the time a stone was ordered for Fannie's grave, the truth was revealed about Lon's background.

Her tombstone has her original birth name of Fannie B. Hussey at the top. The rest of the text reads:

dau(ghter) of B. & W.E. Hussey
and beloved wife of
Alonzo Maxwell
DIED
June 13, 1881
AGED
17 Ys. 2 Ms. 26 Ds.

On the lower quarter of the stone is a note that begins "Dear Fannie." Unfortunately time and the weather have rendered the message unreadable. Since we can assume that the stone was not ordered by Lon, the text inscription was probably written by her mother. Fannie, an only surviving child was no doubt her mother's delight. It's significant to note though that the name "Williams" does not appear on Fannie's marker. Instead Lon's true surname is used.

Fannie was laid to rest beside a sister who had died several years before on July 16, 1869 at the age of seven. Her sister's marker is broken exactly where her name appeared rendering it unreadable, but the text clearly states she is the daughter of William and Bridget Hussey. Like Fannie's marker, it too bears an inscription on the lower part.

Fannie's gravestone in Waubeek Cemetery between Durand and Eau Galle, Wisconsin. The six-line inscription on the bottom is no longer legible. It was most likely written by her mother, Bridget Thompson.

Photo: Les Kruger

William Thompson signed an affidavit July 11, 1881 that said Alonzo had visited at his home on Sunday June 26. Bridget Thompson swore in her statement that Lon had come to her house on Friday. She claimed that Lon "just cried like a baby all night about his wife…" when he learned of Fannie's death. Grief stricken, Lon spent the night over his wife's grave. The following day they borrowed Mr. Downer's team of horses and Mrs. Thompson and Lon rode to Hersey. There they cleaned out the house that Fannie and Alonzo had called home. The two remained there for the night and the next day Bridget's husband arrived and drove them all back to the Thompson home in Arkansaw. On the way Alonzo made a stop in Menonomie. At Conway and Anderson's emporium, he had a black hat trimmed with crepe to indicate he was in mourning. Bridget was to say later that she would not be able to recognize it because Lon always wore a hat. The next day William drove Lon to Pepin. Knowing he was being hunted by the law and that Under Sheriff Knight was planning to come to arrest him, he decided to leave so as to not cause any more trouble for the Thompsons. Before departing however, he told Bridget that he would be back by October to "fix up his wife's grave". Later circumstances prevented him from completing that mission.

Lon's visit to Hersey did not go unnoticed. One of his neighbours saw Lon and Bridget retrieving several household effects from Fannie and Lon's former home there. The neighbour had a conversation at that time with Lon. According to the man, Lon said, "When I got married and settled down in Hersey, I intended to lead an honorable and upright life. I took a contract for cutting cordwood and worked faithfully till my brother arrived from prison and put hell into me. I would give all of St. Croix County to be back where I was last winter, but the game is up. My wife is dead. We are fugitives from justice, and we have made up our minds never to be taken alive."

The neighbour also claimed that before leaving Hersey, Lon approached the telegraph operator, G.W. Reynolds, and begged Reynolds not to notify the authorities of his presence that day in Hersey as a personal favour. (Some reports say that Lon threatened to shoot the man if he didn't comply.) He added, "I have arrived at the point where life is nothing to me, but I want to leave Hersey peaceably, if possible, and I intend to get out of the country for good." Shortly afterwards, Alonzo "Williams" left the village of Hersey for the last time. Bridget Thompson later stated that she had a letter from Lon mailed to her from Bad Axe dated June 29[th,] three days after she last saw him. True to his word, he was then heading away from the Durand area, at least temporarily.

There was one last task with which Lon wanted to deal prior to leaving the region. He needed to set the record straight about his relationship with and love for his wife. Knowing that soon he would not be able to defend his deep feelings for his dead wife, he turned to Elder Downer to unload a burden he was carrying. The note for Downer was relayed from Lon to the cleric by a boy whom Lon paid to deliver his message:

Sunday night, June 26, 1881
Mr. Downer, Sir:

I have been wanting to speak with you ever since I came back, and not having the opportunity I will have to transfer my thoughts to paper. I want to say this (although it isn't much), that what few of the neighbors and acquaintances of mine that respected me in the least when I was first married, I want to keep their respect. I know at the present time that I have very few sympathizing friends. The majority doubtless say I pitied his wife, but HIM – let him go to the dogs.

Now as far as I am concerned, I want to say this – that when folks say about me I don't care so much as this: The talk was started that I married Fanny with the intentions of leaving her. I want to say that no man was ever more honest in dealing with or profession to a woman than I was with her. Circumstances placed me in such position that I could hear nothing of the way things were agoing up here till I finally came up. But too late. She was dead.

Oh, this has been a terrible shock to me, although few believe it. They doubtless say this, "He is glad of it;" but, Mr. Downer, you had better buried me than her, for I now am a ruined man. My life is wrecked and I care no more for it. I was always alone in the world till I got her, and now I stand alone again, with nothing to live for and no object in view.

It almost sets me crazy when I hear of anyone saying, "He intended to leave her in the spring anyway." But, Mr. Downer, if my word is good for anything believe what I have said. It can now make no difference to me what people say, only it seems as though I had ought to say it for her sake but not my own. I know she was too good a woman for me; I knew it but still I know as well how to appreciate her as anyone could, and now that she is dead I want to clear her memory of every chance of reproach because she was as innocent as any angel could be; and now, Mr. Downer, she has been torn from me, it might have been the will of God, but I think it was the doings of men, and my desire to retaliate is fearful strong – nothing but respect for her holds me back; but now if they come for me again I won't run for them.

I have nothing to keep me out of their way for. When Fannie was alive I kept out of their way for her sake, but now they have done all they could; they have driven me away from her, and I'll never see her again now. All they can do is come and take my life, they can take it easy if they know how. Mr. Downer, my life is so wrecked that I almost want them to come on to me that they can see what a desperate wreck they have left. Now, Mr. Downer, I simply tell you all this because I know you to be a man of principle. I mean this just for yourself, and if justice were done me, no charge would be brought against me. I merely wanted to help my brother, and that ruined me. If it is not asking too much of you, I wish you would pray for me. A petition to God from some one, for I can't do it myself. Farewell.

Respectfully
    L. D. Williams

The letter clearly suggested several things about the state of mind Lon was in at the time. It was a strongly worded declaration of love and devotion for his deceased loved one. It also revealed the degree of despondency to which he had succumbed. He sensed that his life was as ruined then as it was before he met and married her.

But most disturbing was his use of the word "they" in attempting to attach blame for Fannie's death. Referring to it as the "doings of men" he flatly stated that "... if they come for me ... I won't run from them". This could only be intended to refer to the law. And then he all but issued a challenge: "I almost want them to come."

And inevitably, they did come. In Alonzo's frame of mind, the outcome could only have murderous consequences.

Both Bridget and William Thompson swore in affidavits at the Colemans' inquest that Alonzo spent nights in this cemetery weeping over Fannie's grave. She rests to the right of the entrance. Photo: Les Kruger

The COLEMAN MURDERS

MILTON COLEMAN, UNDERSHERIFF OF Dunn County, had travelled to Wabasha to pick up a prisoner about 18 miles south of Durand, accompanied by Undersheriff Miletus Knight of Pepin County. John C. Walker had stolen some watches and jewelry from Toft's store in Menonomie where Coleman was based, and was apprehended in Wabasha. Milton made the trip there to pick up the thief and return him for a court appearance in Menonomie. Mr. Toft had accompanied Milt to identify his property. They returned to Knight's home-town of Durand where the suspect was placed in jail to hold him until the following morning when they would continue on to Menonomie.

Milton had an ulterior motive for wanting the lay-over. His brother Charles, who had been sheriff of Pepin County the previous term, lived in Durand. Meeting Milt at the jail, which was conveniently located in a building adjacent to the Durand Court House, the two were making ready for a social evening. Knight had already returned home to his family for supper, but Charles and Milton looked forward to a brotherly visit. It was Sunday, July 10th, 1881.

Milton Coleman: Under-Sheriff
from Menonomie of Dunn County

Late that same afternoon, Frank Goodrich had met two men on the west side of the Chippewa River as they made their way towards Durand. They asked Goodrich about the exact location of the jail and in particular about whether Miletus Knight would be at the jail or in the vicinity. Knight had recently recovered a stolen horse. It's been assumed that these men were going to try to reclaim it, but their mission was unquestionably much more personal than that.

Arriving at the river, they met William Goodrich, the ferry operator at Durand, and had him take them across the Chippewa to the town side about six o'clock. Goodrich wasn't certain at first, but began to suspect that these two were the "Williams" brothers. They certainly matched the descriptions, especially when he noted the arms they were carrying. It wasn't hunting season. He hurried to the Sheriff's office at the jail to inform the authorities of his suspicions.

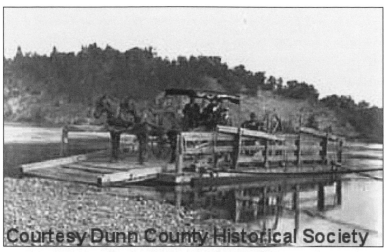

This ferry on the Chippewa River was similar to the one used by the Maxwells to cross into Durand. Each would hold up to two vehicles and several horses and passengers.

Weeks before, Sheriff Anderson in Illinois had sent out postal cards to as many law enforcement agencies as he could. The cards bore the photos of each of the Maxwell boys and were inscribed with a warning, "Be careful and go armed, they are desperate men". One of the recipients of those cards was Milton. He was fully aware of the scoundrels and the extra reward money for their capture.

J. O. ANDERSON.

If this story has a "hero" to it, it would have to be Sheriff James Oscar Anderson of Oquawka in Henderson County, Illinois. Not only did he alert other law enforcement agencies about the Maxwells, he also made a point of offering his services further by attending personally in Wisconsin at the manhunt. He was that kind of dedicated lawman. His county voted him into the position five consecutive terms. James had always been a person with a conscience. He enlisted in the Union in the Illinois Infantry as soon as he was allowed by age. At 18 he was fighting in the front lines. After the war's end, he remained with his regiment and was sent to Texas under General Phil Sheridan as part of the "Army of Observation" to oppose the forces of Maximilian in Mexico. He mustered out of service in 1866 with the rank of First Sergeant. Later as a sheriff, he tended his law enforcement with the same style of military precision to which he had become accustomed.

Milton and Charles Coleman prepared themselves to take up the hunt. Miletus Knight was already home for supper and there seemed no reason to disturb him for the arrest. Armed each with a revolver and a double-barreled shotgun, the Colemans set out towards the area where the "Williams" had been last seen. But their preparations were inadequate considering the outcome. Their shotguns were loaded with only light birdshot, a mistake which would contribute to the outcome.

The main street of Durand ran roughly parallel to the river for about a half mile before taking a slight turn away from the river, then the street forked. The northeast fork went to Eau Claire. The other branched east to Mondovi. The fork was close to the vicinity where William Goodrich had deposited the Maxwells from his ferry. The Colemans, carrying their shotguns in their hands, made their way towards the Mondovi/ Eau Claire fork. They asked several citizens along the route whether anyone had seen two armed men in the vicinity. Without realizing it, the two lawmen had actually got ahead of the Maxwells who were now behind them.

Area of the Chippewa River at Durand close to where the Maxwells crossed near the Dorchester place at the Mondovi/ Eau Claire fork. Today a new bridge built in 2006 for Highway 10 spans this stretch of river. Photo: Les Kruger

The late afternoon was now turning to dusk. Near the turn-off to Mondovi on the front porch of a house owned by J. T. Dorchester, sat two boys, one about 14 years old. His brother was somewhat younger. They crossed their lawn coming out to the gate to speak to the Coleman brothers. The older, Tallie Dorchester, said that they had not seen anyone matching the descriptions. Just then Milton Coleman looked down the street toward the village and saw two men walking side by side and coming towards them.

While Charles was speaking to the boys, Milt said, "Hush, there they are now." Both Colemans cocked their guns. Milton was standing near the fence. Charles stepped about six feet into the roadway and slightly behind Milton.

The melee which transpired next is recorded from the description given by the two boys who were so close to the action that several of the bullets passed within three feet of their heads. The entire action took only a few seconds.

As the two sets of brothers got within 15 to 20 feet of each other, Milt threw his shotgun to his shoulder aiming it directly at Alonzo and yelled, "You are my ----"

The sentence was never finished. Before Milt could add the word "prisoner", Lon Maxwell fired his revolver with deadly accuracy hitting Milton Coleman in the neck killing him almost instantly. The bullet hit the left side of the neck, tore through the jugular vein and several arteries, and broke the bones in his neck. It exited at the back, just right of center. He was probably dead before hitting the ground.

As an added insurance, Alonzo fired a second bullet that only grazed the lawman's cheek as he fell. But Milton had fired a shot too. Whether his finger pulling the trigger was a muscular reaction to the shock of being shot, or whether he did have a split second reaction to the situation, he managed to unload one barrel of his birdshot that hit Alonzo in the face and arm. As Milton slumped onto the road, Lon quickly retreated in the direction from which he had come.

While this gun-battle was raging, Charles Coleman and Ed Maxwell were squaring off in their corner. Almost simultaneously, they shot at each other. Ed was hit in the arm and hand by a blast of Charles' birdshot, but not before Maxwell was able to deal Coleman a fatal shot. The only witnesses guessed that Ed fired five or six times. Probably he emptied his revolver. Charles was hit twice. The bullet that killed him struck him in the chest just below his heart. The other tore through his right arm near the shoulder smashing the bone. Ed had fired many shots at Charles but most had missed as Coleman deliberately tried to avoid them by dashing further out into the road writhing to thwart Maxwell's aim. Sinking down onto one knee after being hit, Charles fired at Ed a second time. He was still breathing when Tallie Dorchester reached him. He died very soon afterwards in the street where he collapsed. The young Dorchester boy watched Charles give his last gasp.

Ed Maxwell walked away briskly and joined his brother where Lon waited near the corner. The two then disappeared into the night. The Maxwells were spotted easily by the Colemans probably because they were carrying their Winchester rifles. But the shooting most likely came from their revolvers. This was probably because they required less time to aim and fire. Alonzo and Ed had practiced long and often shooting at marks, and both were reputed to be deadly shots with either their handguns or their rifles. This they demonstrated in the early evening of July 10th, 1881.

Both Colemans lay dead in the street, Milton near the Dorchester fence; Charles in the center of the roadway.

Charles Coleman:
Former Sheriff in Durand
of Pepin County

Blood splattered on the boards for several feet along the fence, was testimony that Alonzo was wounded during the gunfight, even if only slightly. The absence of any ejected rifle shells on the street was proof that the Maxwells had used pistols rather than their Winchesters. The only other interesting item at the scene was Alonzo Maxwell's hat described as "a low round-crowned hat with a band of crape (sic) around it". For a minute or two, the only sound was the quiet of the evening.

Having heard the rapid and heavy gunfire in their neighborhood, people rushed out of their homes anxious to know what happened.

For some, the gunfight outside left them to talk about a slightly more personal involvement in the action. The two Dorchester boys had the scenario branded into their memories for the remaining decades of their lives. Mr. and Mrs. William Perkins were just preparing to retire for the evening when their window was shattered by an errant bullet from a Maxwell revolver. The projectile lodged itself in the wall over their bed startling the elderly couple. It was several hours later before they were again able to get back into bed.

The other neighbours became spectators to a scene of graphic gore and horror, their eyes riveted to the gruesome tableau before them. The sight of the dead lawmen lying in pools of their own blood, testimony to the unparalleled tragedy on their street, was at first received with quiet, reserved shock. For a few brief minutes they dared do little more than survey the scene. The women stood off to the side, their hands clasped over their mouth; some of the men walked close to the bodies, and then shook their heads as they looked away. There would be no touching the Colemans. It was obvious the two men were dead. Someone sent a messenger to summons Sheriff Peterson and Under-Sheriff Knight. At first, all the gathering crowd could do was to stare and wonder who could be responsible for such a bloodbath, and why. But their shock and horror were soon given over to anger that quickly escalated to outrage. Both Coleman brothers were known widely in the community and were well liked and respected. Such carnage was not going to be tolerated.

Within hours, a posse was organized that would begin the largest manhunt in Wisconsin's history.

This was the main street of Durand, Wisconsin in 1881. The painting
was done by Frank S. Stewart in that year. Courtesy Pepin County Historical Museum

The COLEMAN FUNERALS

THE BODIES OF MILTON and Charles were removed from the street where they had been murdered, and taken to the home of Mr. Martin Maxwell. Because Ed and Lon were known as "Williams" in the Durand area at the time, no one would have noticed the irony of the Colemans being borne to the residence of a Maxwell. However, they were taken there because the Colemans' sister, Mary, was married to Martin Maxwell, a respected local businessman who dealt in lumber, and no relation to Ed or Alonzo.

The funeral was held at nine in the morning just two days after the shootings. It was the biggest funeral ever held in the area with people present from both Durand and Menonomie. The Reverend John Steele from Menonomie conducted the service with assistance from Reverend W. C. Ross and Reverend G.D. Brown.

In the parlor of the Maxwell house the two open caskets lay side by side. People filed past one last time to pay their final respects to the two officers. Family members were present rendering it a difficult and sad time. It was said that Alice Coleman, the boys' mother, bore the strain well under the circumstances. Later she collapsed from exhaustion and grief, and was placed under a doctor's care.

Although the two men were together one last occasion for their funerals, their burials were miles apart. Charles was buried in the Durand Cemetery following a brief ceremony conducted by the Durand Lodge of Masons. The Durand Brass Band escorted the cortege to the grave-site playing a dirge during the mournful procession.

Charles left behind a wife and seven children. Since receiving a serious head wound suffered at the Battle of Perryville during the Civil War, Charles had a difficult time maintaining a full-time job. Consequently, debts had mounted and he struggled financially. At the time of his death he still owed a hundred dollars on his house. He had tried to apply to take out a life insurance policy at least twice, but because of the nature of his infirmity, no company would insure him. According to the minutes of a special meeting held after the funeral on the 12th of July, a motion was carried that his lodge pay all the costs incurred by Charles' funeral.

Charles' grave in Durand Cemetery. Although the wording is weathered and faint, the inscription at the bottom reads: He died at his post. The small star marker indicates he served in the Civil War for the GAR (Grand Army of the Republic.) His parents, Alice and Henry Coleman, are buried in a plot adjacent to his Photo: Les Kruger

Leaving behind so many dependents without a benefactor was a hardship that did not go unnoticed by his friends. Within a matter of weeks the newspapers were calling for a collection to be taken up in support of Charles' family. Neighbors and friends responded with numerous donations of money, baskets of food and sides of beef and pork. Charles' wife and children were not going to be in despair as long as people could manage to help them. The Honorable William Carson, about two weeks after the killings, proposed that the town "raise by subscription" a substantial fund to support Charley's wife and her family in the future. Being the first to offer the idea, he was also the first to offer a donation putting $25 into the pot. The donations aided greatly in giving the family some much needed financial security. Ironically, Charles earned more for his family in death than he was able to provide in life.

Milton Asa Coleman's remains were removed to Menonomie by his fellow I.O.O.F. (Independent Order of OddFellows) Lodge members where he laid in state at the court-house to allow his fellow citizens a last opportunity to pay their respects. Over a thousand people came for a final chance to view the man they admired and respected. Reverend Steele stated at the funeral that Milton "…died in your defense". Of Milt's character, the reverend called him "…one that was too brave and too generous to suppose there was such wickedness in the world as that by which he lost his life."

That same evening, he was taken to Evergreen Cemetery, but there were so many men already on their way to join the search for the Maxwells, that the burial had to wait until the following day. Milton was not married, but left behind a young lady, Miss Rosa Nott, a school teacher in Menonomie. She and Milton had planned to be married in the coming fall. At the time of his death, Milt had an insurance policy for $1,000 with his mother named as beneficiary. Both his personal and professional life had looked promising for Milton. All this was cut short by the gunfight in the streets of Durand.

It was said of him that no county ever had a "more faithful, vigilant, efficient and conscientious officer than Milton Coleman. He was a man of exemplary character, sterling integrity and won the friendship and esteem of all by his quiet and unobtrusive manners, genial ways and strict devotion to duty."

Milton A. Coleman's headstone.
Photo: L. Kruger

His tombstone makes no mention of the circumstances of his death. The inscription reads simply:

MILTON A.
Son of
H & A.
COLEMAN
Died
July 10, 1881
AGED
25 Ys 8 Ms
21 Ds

Although it has four sides to it, the marker bears no other inscriptions on the other three sides. Over the years, it has become slanted as the earth gave way under its weight. Although a century and a quarter later the tombstone is in need of leveling and cleaning, in its day the stone would have been selected for the beauty of its simplicity. It marked the resting place of a man who was sorely missed by his family and the town which he served so faithfully.

The tombstone that graced Charles' final resting place in the Durand Cemetery did offer one hint of his demise. Without elaborating on the circumstances, it read, "He died at his post". Over time the lettering is no longer sharp and clear, but the words are still legible. At the time of his death, Charlie was 40 years old. He lies to the left of a small plot now occupied by his mother, Alice, who lived for another ten years after her two sons, and his father, Henry, who passed away in 1869.

Milton and Charles Coleman's parents rest in Durand Cemetery next to Charles' grave. Photo: L. Kruger

The entire Coleman family was highly regarded by the two communities now linked in sorrow. Expressions of sympathy poured in from the outlying villages as well. Most expressed their shock and sorrow simply. This item appeared in the Menonomie newspaper:

> The Fall City people feel deeply the murder of Milton Coleman
> who was well known here and highly respected.

The Lodges to which the brothers belonged, as well as several others wishing to offer their heartfelt support, published items of condolences. Some had gone so far as to call special meetings of their membership. There was almost no one in the two towns who was not touched by the deaths. The murders were almost the sole topic of conversation for weeks afterwards. Many of the men joined posses hunting the "Williams" boys. Ladies baked or made sand- wiches for the menfolk to eat on the hunt trail. The effort to bring the killers to justice was a community response.

The support and generosity of the villages were not lost on the Coleman family. Even in her most dire time of grief, the brothers' mother cared enough to publish her own message of thanks:

> We desire to express our heartfelt thanks to our friends and the community in general for the many tokens of respect manifested for our precious dead, and for their sympathy with us in our great sorrow. Mrs. Alice Coleman and Family

The COLEMAN INQUESTS

CHARLES' AND MILTON'S REMAINS were still warm when the legal proceedings kicked into action. Miletus Knight and Sheriff A.F. Peterson were very busy people for the next few hours in particular. After the Colemans' bodies were borne to the home of their sister and brother-in-law, Dr. Hunt was immediately summoned. There was really nothing for the physician to do but pronounce the men officially dead. His recorded verification was short, but blunt: "Saw the bodies of Chs. and Milton they were dead --- gunshot wounds produced the death." It was signed D.W. Hunt.

After dispensing with the formality of the men's death, effort was made to determine how and why the shootings occurred. Since it was known who was involved in the killings, it was reasonable to start with relatives and acquaintances of the murderers.

The Justice of the Peace, A.W. Hammond, summoned William and Bridget Thompson to appear in his office to determine what they knew regarding the shooting and the shooters. Obviously Hammond too was visibly shaken by the events. (He inadvertently summoned the Thompsons to his office at 1 pm on the 10th day of July rather than the 11th. His small error no doubt reflected his shock at the news of the loss to the local justice system.)

There is, however, some mystery about one other of Hammond's transactions. A handwritten document issued as a "complaint" re-

80

ferred to the stolen horse and buggy concealed at the Thompson residence. This complaint preceded a search warrant being issued. It was signed by both Hammond and Miletus Knight. What makes the document intriguing is that it was signed on July 10th 1881, the same day the Colemans were gunned down. It was a Sunday. Was Hammond working extra hours over the weekend? Did Knight sign the document before he left to attend in Wabasha with Milt Coleman? Did he have prior knowledge of the Maxwells in the proximity on that date and was looking for a reason to check out the Thompson place? Thompson said that the Maxwells arrived on June 26. How then did they secret the horse and carriage there on June 25th? There were many questions left unanswered about that particular paper.

There is another possible explanation. The suggestion of a stolen horse and buggy at the Thompson home may have been a ruse to gain access to the premises to determine if Ed and Lon were hiding out there. That would explain why the complaint was dated July 10th. It hardly seems likely that, besides the unit stored at Mrs. Senz' place, there was a second horse and buggy. Certainly the Maxwells did not appear to have transportation. Lon and Bridget had to borrow Mr. Downer's carriage to go to Hersey to clean out their home. The next day Mr. Thompson had to drive Lon to Pepin. It doesn't appear probable that a second stolen horse and buggy ever existed except as an "investigative" stunt concocted by Miletus Knight with some assistance from the bench. After all, the document was nebulously worded as a "complaint". Also to be noted was the absence of any name on the document indicating to whom the phantom horse and buggy belonged. Surely if someone was complaining about their vehicle being stolen, they would have made sure their name was distinct. There does not seem to be any verification that the issuance of a search warrant was ever carried out. It could be that a cursory check of the Thompson house was done to determine that the Maxwells were not hiding there. Perhaps the Thompsons, by their willingness to appear for the inquest, were forthright enough to deflect any complicity on their part by harbouring the murderers.

The Thompsons did show up in Hammond's office the day following the shootout. Most of the information forthcoming from them came down to the fact that they did not know the Maxwell boys all that well. William stated that he had been acquainted with them for less than a year having known them only since "last winter". He had last seen Lon at his house "last Sunday". Since Thompson didn't say "yesterday", it's assumed that he meant Sunday July 3rd. According to Thompson's statement, "that was the first he knew his wife was dead." Obviously Mr. Thompson was mistaken because Lon's letter to Elder Downer was dated June 26th and he was aware of Fannie's death then.

On a second page of his statement, he corrects himself saying, "This should have been a week previous to the 4th of July instead of one week ago." On that occasion he had seen Lon practicing his marksmanship by target shooting. "Lon always has one revolver.", he said. "Every time they (Maxwells) came at my house they had repeating rifles and revolvers… I heard him say he would not be taken alive." Using Thompson's imperfect memory about the dates, the week before July 4th would be approximately June 26th when Lon wrote the Downer letter. Thompson also said that Lon stayed at his house on the Sunday night and the next morning he drove Lon to Pepin.

Most of this information is confirmed by Bridget Thompson. She had received a letter from Lon post-marked from Bad Axe on the 29th, two days after her husband drove Lon to Pepin. She said she hadn't seen them for almost a month, but when she did see them, it was before the 4th of July. She described both men in her statement indicating that Lon had light brown hair but his whiskers were black because he coloured them. Whether this was a fashion statement of Lon's at the time or an attempt to disguise himself, she did not elaborate.

It's curious to note that she never called Ed by name. When not referring to him as part of the plural "they" or "the boys", she alludes to him as "the other". William did exactly the same. Using Ed's name only once, Thompson preferred to refer to him as "the brother". Neither used the name "Maxwell", but instead called them the "Williams" brothers.

The testimony of the Thompsons was not only heard by Hammond, but also witnessed by William Bachelder of Durand. Besides acknowledging that he witnessed the Thompsons' statements, he also swore that he saw two strangers whom he believed to be the Williams brothers in Durand on the previous evening. They were near the sawmill carrying "long guns". As part of the inquest, Bachelder viewed the dead bodies of the Colemans and claimed to have seen that Charles had been shot in the chest and Milton shot in the neck.

A brief side-note on names: For whatever reasons, the paperwork leaving the desk of Mr. Hammond in his official capacity of Justice of the Peace, was addressed to the Thompsons at the "town of Waterville" in Pepin County. This was the case for both the document about the stolen horse and buggy and the summons to appear in his office. But the Thompsons had moved from Hersey to Arkansaw which, according to Fannie's obituary, was where she died.

When the issue of changing the venue of the county seat came before the voters, the Pepin Courier on November 11, 1881 referred to the proposed alternative as "Arkansaw" not "Waterville". The usage of the word "town" was more political than geographical. The village was called Arkansaw; the area around it, including the village, was the "town" of Waterville. The name fluctuated according to who used it for what purpose. Today there is no Waterville in Pepin County on the map of Wisconsin although a Waterville Township survives southeast of Arkansaw.

Courtesy Pepin County Historical Society

Pepin County Town of Durand To William Thompson and Mrs. William Thompson you are hereby required to appear before the undersigned of the Justice of the Peace in and for said County at my office in Durand on the 10th day of July 1881 at 1, o'clock in the afternoon of said day, to give evidence in a certain inquest then and there to be held over the bodies of Charles Coleman and Milton Coleman now lying dead at the house of M. Maxwell in said town.

Given under my hand this 10th day of July 1881
A.W. Hammond
Justice of the Peace

Copy of the summons sent to William and Bridget Thompson to appear before the Justice of the Peace following the killing of the Coleman brothers.

Courtesy Pepin County Historical Society

Photocopy of original transcript seeking a search warrant to examine the Thompson property for a stolen buggy and horse. It's curious that this document is dated on the same day that the Colemans were killed, in fact, a Sunday. What's even stranger is that Miletus Knight was away from Durand that day attending in Wabash with Milt Coleman.

State of Wisconsin Pepin County Makes a complaint on oath and says, that on the 25 day of June 1881, in said county, divers goods and chattels of the said,

To wit, one horse and buggy were feloniously stolen, taken away carried away by some person or persons unknown and he has good reason to believe that the said goods and chattels or some part of them are concealed on the premises of William Thompson situated in the town of Waterville in said county and he prays that a search warrant be forthwith issued, to search the aforesaid premises for said property. Subscribed and sworn before me, and complain and examined this 10th day of July 1881 M. Knight A.W. Hammond Justice of the Peace

The WAR and CHARLIE COLEMAN

LYING DEAD IN HIS sister's home in Durand, Ex-Sheriff Charles seemingly was just another dead lawman shot in the line of duty. Death has a way of factoring people so that as they lie in their boxes waiting for burial, they all seem to be somewhat equal; just another soul waiting a turn to knock at Heaven's Gate.

But Charles G. Coleman was so much more than just another name waiting to be added to the roster of the dead. In life he had character, personality. He had always been something of a free spirit. And he was loved by his family for all those endearing qualities he embodied.

When the War Between the States broke out, Charles and his family lived in Maxville, about ten miles south of Durand. Alice and Henry raised four sons and two daughters. Mary was the oldest child. Charles was the oldest son followed by Edward, Milton and Henry. Their sister Sarah Jane, was younger than Charles and Edward, but older than the other two boys. The family was close-knit and well-mannered. Their work ethic was passed down from the elder Coleman who had been self-employed for many years as a blacksmith in Bloomington, Illinois.

Some years after the Durand tragedy, somewhere around 1887, Sarah was requested to outline some personal history regarding

Charles and a series of events involving her that took place during the war. She remembered the adventure quite vividly.

Charles was one of five recruits from that area who answered the call of the president for volunteers shortly after the war broke out. His two younger brothers helped him convince their parents to allow him to enlist. Respect for his parents was such that he would not sign up without their blessings. It was granted and he went to Wyocena where he was registered in Company "D" of the 10th Wisconsin Volunteers.

Before he left home for service, Sarah extracted a promise from him that if he were to be wounded or sick, he would let her know by mail or by message and that she would come to him. In those days they received mail twice a week and on each delivery day they would anxiously look forward to any communication from Charles, hoping for a letter telling them not only of the progress of the military activities, but also of his safety and well-being.

The 10th Wisconsin saw several brief skirmishes in the early weeks and months. As he had promised, Charles wrote home frequently with tales of the exploits of his regiment. The war was still young but the fighting was fierce. The 10th performed with distinction, winning praise from the top brass. But their biggest battle awaited them at Perryville, Kentucky. Also known as the Battle of Chaplin Hills, it was fought on October 8, 1862.

Charles' regiment was placed under the leadership of Colonel Harris in the Ninth Brigade which in turn was put in General Rousseau's division. Reaching Maysville the night of October 7th, the troops slept, then marched the next morning until they arrived about two miles outside Perryville

It was to be the largest battle of the war fought on Kentucky soil. General Braxton Bragg's 18,000 Confederate troops were assembled on the fields and farmland facing 58,000 Union troops under the command of Major General Don Carlos Buell. The odds against the Rebels were mathematically overwhelming, but strange things can happen when over-confidence gives way to poor judgment. When the Battle of Perryville was over, more than 7,500 soldiers from both sides would lie in those same fields dead or wounded.

Truth is often found in strange places. One Civil War soldier found dead on a battlefield had a letter to his family in his pocket. It was discovered when he was being prepared for burial. In it he had written, "When Generals make mistakes, they lose their reputations, their soldiers lose their lives." Nothing could have more aptly described the Battle of Perryville. Buell, with a far superior number of forces, chose to hold back almost two-thirds from the battle. The end result was that, of those he used, a heavy proportion was lost either through death or injuries, not to mention the field equipment and horses. Bragg, for his part, lost his nerve. Tactically, he won the battle. Instead of capitalizing on his victory by following up with a rout of the federals that night or the next day, he chose instead to slink back to Tennessee during the night, creating instead a hollow success for his forces. Winning a retreat forfeits any victory.

If the battle was terrible, its aftermath was worse. In retreating, the Confederates left behind on the field its dead and dying. This from a Union cavalryman the next morning:

> We found that the Rebels had left during the night. We marched over the battlefield. It was a horrible sight. For four miles the fields are strewn with the dead of both parties, some are torn to pieces and some in the dying agonies of death The ambulances are unable to take all the wounded ... A large pile of legs and arms are lying around that the rebel doctors cut off.

On the morning of the Perryville battle, Charles Coleman's 10th Wisconsin Regiment was one of several lined up on the crest of a hill facing the Rebels who were assembled along the ridge of an opposing hillside. The 10th was 360 men strong with 16 officers. About 11 o'clock they had been ordered to support a battery under the command of a Captain Simmons. They remained positioned behind the cannons until about 3 in the afternoon. Until that time they had sustained only four wounded. They were ordered to advance to an-

other ridge at the double-quick only to discover the enemy advancing also several lines deep. The advancing Confederates continued
forward, at times seeming to be confused enough to charge right on
past the Union ranks.

This is the exact position of the Wisconsin 10th at Perryville battlefield.
Charles would have been wounded within feet of where this cannon
now stands. Photo: Les Kruger

Volley after volley were fired at the enemy until finally they were
repulsed. But the Rebels soon regrouped and once more charged the
ridge held by the 10th. By now the fray was an exercise in a brutal
attempt to survive. Soldiers dropped like flies as the cannons blazed
and the rifles fired. It became difficult to gain traction on the slopes
for the blood that was running downhill. Men didn't simply drop
from the shots they received; they frequently were blown apart.
Limbs and body parts were scattered over the battleground. A soldier wrote about seeing one poor devil whose entire lower jaw was
completely shot away leaving his tongue to dangle in the gore. Others were totally blinded and floundering on the hillsides.

They fought until their ammunition was exhausted. Then they

raided the cartridge boxes of the dead and injured to find more. For almost a half hour, the 10th fought off the enemy with almost no ammunition, but managed to hold their position until finally supported by the 38th Indiana Regiment. A short time later they were ordered to retreat back to the ridge behind them. Throughout the battle the regimental flag never stopped flying despite several of the colour-bearers being shot down. Forty-one bullets passed through the flag and two more went through its shaft. When the cannons and rifles were finally silenced, from the fields and hills came the sickening moaning of the dying and wounded.

The 10th sustained a death toll of 48 both on the field and of those who died soon afterwards as a result of their wounds. Ninety-seven others were officially listed as wounded. One of those was Charles Coleman.

Still showing signs of blood stains, this billfold was carried by Charles through the war and his ordeal at Perryville. It was made for him by his sister, although it's not clear which one. The note was inside the cloth billfold. The text reads: This is to certify that Bro. Charles Coleman has been an exceptible (sic) member of the M.E. Methodist Church at Max-ville. Aug. 3, 1861. M. Woodley, Pepin

His family learned of his situation the toughest way possible.

They were given a neighbour's newspaper that reported the tragedy at Perryville with a list of the injured. Beside the name, Charles Coleman, it read "seriously, and perhaps fatally wounded in the head." Sarah wrote that on reading those words, "our faces blanched as each in turn examined the list, and read over and over the fearful words." In the evening as the family sat around the fireplace, the elder Henry Coleman committed the fate of Charles to the Almighty and asked Him to bless their son and return him home safely. That night, unable to sleep, Sarah formulated a plan in her mind. She was determined to go and find her brother wherever and in whatever condition she could locate him. Anticipating some protestations from her parents, she was surprised the next morning when they offered nothing but support for her venture.

By noon she was on her journey to search for her brother. Henry Sr. took her by buggy to Durand where she caught a steamboat down the Chippewa to Wabasha on the Minnesota side of the Mississippi. From there she ferried down to La Crosse where she remained overnight. The next day Sarah took a train to Minnesota Junction where she then made the first of several train changes before reaching her destination. Traveling through Chicago, Michigan City and La Fayette, Indiana, she eventually reached Louisville where she put up at a hotel. For a young lady to move about on her own so far from home during such turbulent times was certainly an heroic exhibition of bravery.

Courtesy P.M. O'Brien from Spring Brook Saga

One of the last stage coaches in Wisconsin about 1870.

It was not going to be easy to locate Charles. The numbers of wounded, not only from the Perryville battle, but from skirmishes fought throughout the various engagements were in the thousands. It was impossible to know just where to begin looking. She began her search through the hospitals in Louisville. It has to be understood that almost any type of building, house, store or stable might have been a "hospital" during those chaotic months. In the immediate area around Perryville after the battle virtually every house, barn or shed was converted to a temporary shelter for the wounded. Many weren't that fortunate and suffered in the chill air outside exposed to the weather. For the moment at least, sanitation was less a concern than was shelter and comfort. Some of the farmhouses were commandeered, others volunteered. In many instances they still held wounded soldiers months after the day of the battle. Around Perryville there might have been thirty or forty "hospitals". Temporary facilities had also been set up in area towns and villages forty and fifty miles away to help house the wounded.

At the seventh hospital she visited, Sarah found Gilbert Dowd, one of the five volunteers who had enlisted with Charles from Durand. He had been wounded in the arm at the same Battle of Perryville. He told Sarah that Charlie was fine; he had seen Charlie carrying water to other soldiers after he had been wounded. This was not satisfactory to Sarah. She needed to see Charles for herself.

Prior to leaving on this journey, Sarah had been given a letter of introduction by Theodore Lewton to his uncle, a Mr. Graham who lived in Louisville. Not finding Graham at home when she visited, Sarah had left her card at his home. Graham later met Sarah at her hotel. He and his daughter took her for a drive during which he advised her that due to the circumstances of the war, she should abandon her search. He said that Major-General Buell's army of a hundred thousand soldiers was ninety miles away at New Market. Seeing Sarah's determination to go anyway, Graham secured for her a pass from General Rousseau who was a personal friend of Graham. He arranged for her to be on a train which would take her to Lebanon, Kentucky just six miles from New Market.

By now Sarah was almost discouraged enough to give up the hunt, but with some trepidation, she boarded the train in the early morning. Although the cars were all full, only one other woman was on the train, a young lady on a similar mission. By 4:00 pm she reached Lebanon. Getting to New Market by 9 that evening, she again planned to stay at a hotel. The village had only two hotels, both full beyond capacity.

Her only alternative was to try to find accommodations at a private residence. After knocking on several doors unsuccessfully, at another she was met by a woman who at first denied her entrance. Claiming the house was full of sick people, she said she had neither room nor food to give the stranger. Sarah asked to share only the privilege of sitting by the fireplace to escape the coolness of the night. Finally after some persuasion, the woman agreed. She was shown to a seat by the fire.

As it turned out, the house belonged to rebels, southern supporters who had no sympathy for the Federals. Besides the first lady Sarah met at the door, there was another sister in the house and a Confederate lieutenant recuperating from being wounded. Nevertheless, they extended their hospitality towards Sarah despite the differences in political support, and offered her some food. In those hard times, it wasn't much, but the best they could offer: coffee without milk or sugar, and fat pork.

By now it was late into the evening, and Sarah was able to get some sleep. In the morning soldiers began coming to the house attempting to secure any supplies. Sarah made inquiries of them as to where she might find the 10th Wisconsin located. She mentioned her brother's name and handed several her card, but nothing positive resulted that would assist her.

On a hunch though, she also inquired about the three other young men who had enlisted with Charles and Gilbert Dowd. There's no officer in any army that can motivate a young man as quickly as can a lady asking for him by name. In short order two of the other friends of Charles appeared to tell her that they had no news of him since the day of the Perryville battle until, coincidentally, the day before Sarah arrived. Only the previous day, John Doughty had received a letter from William Day stating that Charles was badly wounded and lying in a hospital at Perryville. John was a cousin of Charles and Sarah on their mother's side of the family. He had tried to secure a leave of absence to visit Charles, but had been refused. Risking the wrath of the army, he decided to accompany Sarah by taking a "French leave", or in other words, to go with her on the sly.

They found an army wagon heading back to Lebanon. Their plan was to get that far. Sarah had already arranged for a stagecoach for them for the remaining eighteen miles to Perryville. They arrived at their destination about four in the afternoon and immediately began searching. By that time tents had been brought in to help shelter the wounded and they went from one tent to another viewing the sick and wounded, looking for Charles.

In one of these tents John Doughty recognized the writer of the letter, William Day. Day could offer no further information of

Charles' whereabouts. He did know a little of the circumstances of his situation, however. He told them that three days after the battle Charles had been found on the floor of an old tin shop. The door had been blown off its hinges and was lying on top of him. Assuming he was dead, they removed him from the building but in doing so, discovered him to be alive but unconscious. He was transported to a hospital and was placed under the care of Dr. Polk. After examining Charles, Polk said he felt he could do nothing for him. After Charles remained in a coma for two days, Dr. Polk considered that he might live after all. He had been struck in the head by a mini ball and Dr. Polk had thought an operation might be necessary. But before it could be performed, Charlie regained consciousness, asked for food and inquired about his revolver which had been stolen during the battle. After that, he disappeared and no one knew of his whereabouts. Had he been transferred, it would have been recorded.

Dr. Jefferson J. Polk became an unwilling hero of the Perryville Battle. Highly respected in the town, he also doubled as a preacher. He practiced medicine for nineteen years before being forced to retire in 1859 due to failing health resulting from a severe bronchial disease. But with more than 7,500 casualties lying in the fields, Dr. Polk's practice was instantly renewed. Surveying the carnage the next day, he was quickly pressed into service. Years later after his second retirement, he described some of what he saw that day:

> The first hospital I entered was Mr. Peter's house. Here were about two hundred wounded soldiers lying side by side on beds of straw. Notwithstanding they were wounded in every possible way, there was not heard among them a groan or complaint. In the orchard close by a long trench had been dug, in which to bury the dead; about fifteen were lying in a row, ready for internment. ...
>
> I passed on northward, and saw on either hand dead men and dead horses, canteens, muskets, cartridge boxes, broken ambulances, coats, hats and shoes scattered thick over the ground. I reached Mr. Russell's white house... Here was the center of the great battle. The house was dotted with hundreds of marks of musket

and cannon balls. All around lay dead bodies of the soldiers ... In a skirt of woods close by were scattered hundreds of the dead of both armies ...

The ground was strewn with soiled and torn clothes, muskets, blankets, and the various accouterments of the dead soldiers. Trees not more than one foot in diameter contained from twenty to thirty musket-balls and buck-shot put into them during the battle ...

I counted four hundred and ten dead men on a small spot of ground. My heart grew sick at the sight ... I saw dead rebels piled up in pens like hogs. I reached my home, praying to God that I might never again be called upon to visit a battlefield ... For months hundreds of the wounded died every week.

Sarah was able to locate the good doctor and make inquires about her brother. Although not able to provide her with much information, he and his two daughters generously offered her a place to stay at their home. As the hotels were all full and nearly every private house was doubling as a space for the wounded to rest and recuperate, she accepted his offer. His home too had several wounded soldiers. Sarah did not have a restful visit: "I could not eat, although urged to do so, and sleep was out of the question with so much suffering around, and such dreadful stories of the battlefield ..."

Dr Polk's office and house in Perryville where Sarah stayed while searching for Charles. Polk, a retired doctor, reluctantly returned to practice medicine to assist the wounded after the battle. Photo: L. Kruger

John continued to search for Charles until late that night but with no results. The next morning Sarah returned by stagecoach to Lebanon but it was full and John had to walk the twenty miles. As soon as she arrived, Sarah began again hunting for Charles. Checking at every barracks and hospital, she found nothing of the man nor any reference to him on the registers. Exhausted, she returned to the hotel to wait for John.

Train station in center of Lebanon, Kentucky about 1875. Many of these buildings would have served as hospitals following the Battle of Perryville. Charles Coleman was hospitalized nearby.

But what she did not know was that Charles had found her. He had been looking out a window of the second story building in which he was housed across the street from her hotel. Recognizing his sister, he ran downstairs and tried to pass the guards. They in turn tried to keep him in even by threatening him with their bayonets. In Sarah's own words, they knew "… him to be somewhat deranged". Insisting that his sister was out there, they told him to wait until she came to him.

At that moment John walked past the hospital building and noticed the confusion inside. Running across the street to the hotel, he yelled to Sarah, "I've found him! I've found Charlie!" Racing into the hospital building, Sarah sprinted past the guards and into his arms. Grabbing Charles, she pulled him out into the street. The sight didn't go unnoticed by the guards as she heard one remark, "Yes, that's so – that is his sister."

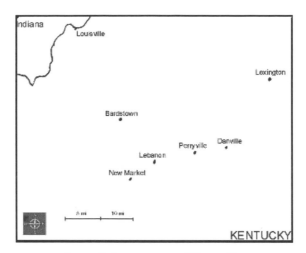

Immediate area around Perryville

She returned to the hospital to get permission to bring Charles across the street to her hotel. The surgeon came also and dressed his wound. She related later about that moment, "I shall never forget the feeling that came over me as I looked upon him. He had a soiled bandage around his head, his hair was matted with blood and his clothes down the side were saturated with it. He wore a short blouse – his overcoat had been stolen, and his pants were frayed out around the bottom and four inches too short, a pair of army shoes out at the toes, and no socks." The doctor put on a fresh dressing and provided him with another suit of clothes. After a bath he put them on.

It didn't take Sarah long to realize that there was something very different about Charles. She said that he was changed to such a degree that she could hardly hold back her tears. "I didn't realize his mental condition."

During their exchange, it was apparent that he had difficulty making conversation. Rather than contribute much to their discussion, he seemed content to let her do the talking, to relate to him about life back home and to speak of friends and acquaintances. He listened to her, but did not ask questions. Finally he said, "Let me ask about Mother, you must let me ask after her." He was to admit later that he could not construct a question. His mind was not functioning well enough to perform that small task.

That night Charles returned to the hospital and Sarah spent the night in the sitting room of the hotel on a cot. John stayed with Charles in the hospital. The next day John left to try to catch up with his regiment which by now had moved. It was the last time she was to ever see her cousin.

Sarah spent part of the day scrounging to get transportation papers for Charles to allow her to take him with her on the train. On that train were two hundred other wounded soldiers. She managed to get him in a car with her without being noticed, but when the conductor came by, he said Charles would have to go to the other car with the rest of the wounded. Pleading her case as only a desperate lady can, Sarah begged that he be left with her. She told the trainman she couldn't bear to be separated from him again. Determining how serious she was, he left them alone in her car.

When they reached Louisville, an officer insisted that Charles not go to a hotel with Sarah, but remain with the soldiers. They were crowded into a shed at the train depot and there they remained until morning. At that time they were to be assigned hospitals. Not willing to leave Charles in case they should again be separated, she remained in the shed with him and the other wounded. This seemed preferable to having to do another search should they lose each other.

But the inevitable happened. When the ambulances came for the soldiers, Charles was taken off to a hospital. Sarah, unable to accompany him, was again left having to track down the hospital to which he was taken. After checking all the hospitals at Louisville, she was sent to New Albany over the Indiana border. She didn't reach there until after four o'clock in the afternoon.

After checking at the fourth hospital, she was told there was no such name on their register, but that a fellow answering his description had been brought in. She was taken to a cot on the upper ward and found Charles lying there unconscious. Noticing Sarah's obvious distress, a gentleman who was visiting another patient said that she would be welcome to stay with him and his wife. Gratefully, she accepted his offer.

Charles remained in a coma for three days. Always at his side during the hours she was allowed in the hospital, Sarah helped nurse him back to health. Placing broth in his mouth, she was able to get him to swallow enough for him to gradually gain strength. At last he regained consciousness and recognized his sister. But his mind was still not functioning as it should. He was agitated and anxious about returning to his regiment. It became his sole preoccupation. His recovery period was slow as he lingered in a weakened state for about a month or six weeks.

Sarah meanwhile was trying to secure a furlough for him. Knowing the cold weather was going to set in and that the river would soon freeze over, she wanted to get the furlough release soon so they could get home before freeze-up.

Without any support from the resident army doctor, Sarah solicited assistance from the post surgeon, a Colonel Fry. Charles' doctor had insisted that Charles was only suffering from a "fissure of the brain", that within a few weeks he'd be ready again for active duty once more on the warfront.

While that doctor and Colonel Fry held an animated discussion in front of the patient, Sarah said that Charlie seemed to be the only disinterested party in the argument. Colonel Fry came out on top of the cause and said Charles could have a leave for twenty-two days. He added however, that he'd be surprised if Charles was ready for action again in twenty-two months. He was right. Charles never again returned to active duty.

His wound to the head was such that Charles was never again completely normal. He had difficulty focusing on things, and as a result seemed unable to hold a job for prolonged periods. Married with seven children, Charles did his best to provide for his family. He had even served a two-year term as Sheriff of Pepin County from 1877 to 1878, but in the two or three years prior to his death he was unable to function well enough to hold a job.

His only property was a "modest homestead" on which there was still an outstanding debt of one hundred dollars. His pension of $24 had been all he had on which to support his family and this was cut off as a result of his death. (The *Dunn County News* reported that Judge Macauley had received notice that the application for an increase in his war pension had been granted as a humanitarian gesture considering the size of his bereaved family. Mrs. Coleman would receive an additional $25 to $50 per month, retroactive to September 1880 until the date of Charles' death. They would be getting more than $200. Ironically the news was reported on October 8, 1881, the anniversary of the Battle of Perryville.)

But Charlie was a popular man in the community of Durand. Being unable to hold a job didn't prevent him from carrying out numerous community–minded projects. One of his favorite contributions was to prepare the cemeteries for Decoration Day. He also led several veteran projects, one of which was to help beautify the cemetery. The day that Ed Maxwell put two bullets into Charles Coleman was not the first time that they both had their names in the same newspaper. Barely a year before, the *Dunn County News* reported on the "Williams" brothers terrorizing the county. That same paper made mention of the popular veteran, Charles Coleman, visiting Menonomie prior to Decoration Day to assist in local ceremonies.

Durand did not forget him in those early days following his death. A memorial fund for the benefit of his family was created with the object of fixing a sum "at least equal the amount of the pension received by him".

His head injury occasionally caused Charlie some grief. Subject to an occasional dizzy or fainting spell, it manifested itself in brief awkward moments that would sometimes spell danger. This short article appeared in the Pepin County *Courier* in August 1880:

> This seems to be Charles Coleman's unlucky season. Only a few days ago he fell into the fire in the blacksmith shop and burnt his face severely, and last Friday he cut his foot nearly off. While chopping a tree down, over the river, the axe glanced and struck his left foot. Commencing at the big toe it split that and then cut a deep

gash clear across the foot. Although not a dangerous wound it will
lay him up for some time.

No doubt the irony of the first sentence is not lost, and in ret-
rospect, somewhat prophetic. The autumn season was certainly not
a good one for him beginning as far back as Perryville. But the coincidence of the cut toe was obvious too when it was recalled that
Lon Maxwell's return to crime came about after he also cut his toe
with an axe.

Almost a year to the day, the Pepin *Courier* of August 19, 1881
offered the following tribute to Charlie:

> Charles Coleman was a model of Christian manhood, a brave,
> true, strong soul, a lofty patriot, a kind, generous, unselfish man
> – whose only enemy was evil. He died as he had lived, facing and
> with undaunted courage, fighting foes of mankind.

The final resting place of Sarah Jane (Coleman) Andrus. Her grave is in
Barker Cemetery near Adair, Illinois.
Photo: Les Kruger

PURSUIT of the MAXWELLS

AN IMMEDIATE CURSORY SEARCH was mounted the night of the shooting with no real expectation of finding the murderers of the Coleman brothers. After all, the Maxwells were in their element. They knew the Eau Galle River bottoms almost as well as any man in the area. They had often prowled the back-roads during their forays, and they knew exactly where to hide and what to avoid. Another advantage they had in their favour was a full moon. By this natural light they were better able to maneuver through the woods and along the river banks for the next few nights. Also, it was generally thought that they had confederates willing to offer them aid. In particular, Edward Wolf and his brothers from Hersey were suspected of abetting them. Wolf was later to react to these accusations.

By the next morning a large posse was being assembled to hunt down the murderers. It was to be the largest ever put together in the State of Wisconsin for a manhunt. It must be remembered that the Maxwell era was barely 15 years after the end of the Civil War. Many of the men in the counties had seen service in their respective militia organizations. They were already toughened men accustomed to danger, darkness and discipline. Many had been shot during the war, some imprisoned, many others simply hardened to shooting and death. They had learned to be cautious, to watch carefully, to read signs for danger. Not a few of these men had risen through the ranks to hold impressive titles, at least during the rebellion. Many had excellent tracking skills and they had good training in firing their weapons. Most importantly, they were willing to shoot at another person. The Maxwells were going to be challenged by men who were quite capable in the field. But Ed and Alonzo were not going to be easy to find.

After the fracas, the Maxwell brothers skirted around Durand on the forested side and then worked their way back to the river. Below the village they found an old skiff, and using a fence board and a shingle, they paddled across the Chippewa. Once across, they walked cross-country to the Eau Galle River, then upstream on that waterway. They wanted to avoid the roads for obvious reasons. Before coming into Durand earlier, they had ridden by horse and buggy which they had left tied in the bush. Reaching this spot about dawn the next morning, they changed out of their blood-soaked clothes into fresh clothing from the buggy, hiding their old ones under a log.

The Eau Galle River Bottoms were thick and difficult to maneuver through. It took a skilled bushman who knew the area to pick his way through the density of the region.
Photo: Les Kruger

Both men had been shot. Lon took the worst of it. His right arm was badly wounded and Ed claimed he picked twenty-six pellets from Lon's upper arm and shoulder. As well, because they had been so close to each other during the firing, Lon's face had powder burns from Milt Coleman's shotgun blast.

Ed's wounds were less severe. Charles had hit him in the wrist and arm with the first shot, but it was enough to cause some damage. Sixteen pellets went through his coat sleeve. Of those, six pierced his arm.

In Menonomie, after the Coleman funeral, a meeting was called in the Concert Hall to raise a posse to hunt for the murderers. Deputy Sheriff E. L. Doolittle led the thirty volunteers to Durand to help take up the chase. A detachment of the Ludington Guards, a cavalry unit based out of Menonomie, also arrived for the manhunt. Their numbers soon swelled to over thirty-five men in the company under the leadership of Captain Thomas George, and Lieutenants G. R. Brewer and H. E. Knapp. The Guards were ordered into the field by the governor of the state, William Smith. He insisted that the Maxwells would be captured if it meant mobilizing all the militia in the entire state.

Chief Officers of the Ludington Guard
Captain Thomas Jefferson George (seated)
2nd Lieutenant Henry Eno Knapp (left)
1st Lieutenant George R. Brewer (right)
Courtesy of Dunn County Historical Society

The *Eau Claire Free Press* stated that the Guard was determined to bring in the killers "dead or alive" and that the posse was manned by a few "old warriors who know how to go at it."

It was estimated that for the first three days fresh recruits were arriving constantly to take up the chase. Men from Knapp and Hersey had also shown up. Many of them would have had no problems recognizing the pair they personally knew as the "Williams" brothers. The Menonomie *News* claimed that by its publication date of July 16, Deputy-Sheriff Doolitle had over one hundred men in his posse. One of those was Edward C. Coleman, brother of Milton and Charles. Of the others, the paper stated they were "…old veteran soldiers who understood their business".

Even the local citizens who were not able to hunt actively contributed in other important ways. This one example appeared in the *News*:

> All persons who are prepared to contribute bread, meat, pickles, tea and coffee to the party in pursuit of the Williams brothers, will leave the articles at the house of S. B. French.

Others joined the hunt because they were close friends of the victims. The Reverend J. E. Webster of Neilsville was a comrade of Charles Coleman. They had both served in Company "D" of the 10th Wisconsin during the war. He attended the funeral and then stayed to join the posse in the hunt for the Maxwells. At the Battle of Perryville he had been standing near Charles when Coleman received the severe head wound. Now he was offering another form of support for his brother-in-arms.

Within a day or two it was estimated that the posse numbers had swelled to over 200. Even Sheriff J. O. Anderson from Illinois came up to help out. Despite being a long way from his own jurisdiction, he felt compelled to add his long-time knowledge of the Maxwells for the benefit of the search leaders.

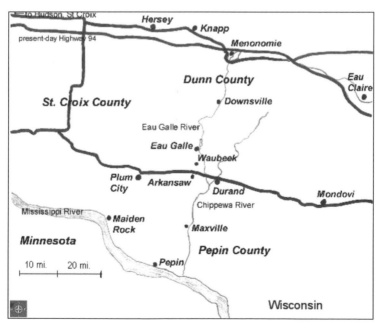

Governor William E. Smith of Wisconsin was notified early in the morning of Monday, July 11th of the lawmen's murder. He immediately set a $500 reward for the capture of the Maxwells. A hurried bulletin was issued from his office the next day:

> The Governor of Wisconsin, by proclamation, issued July 12, 1881, offers a reward of $500 for the arrest and conviction of Alonzo Williams and Ed. Williams, alias "Maxwell", the murderers of Milton Coleman and Charles Coleman, at Durand, Pepin County, Wis.

He also indicated that the equipment and the manpower of the local military company in Menonomie would be available to the law enforcement people in an effort to capture the Maxwells more quickly. In short order a more formal announcement of the reward was sent out to newspapers in the region. This was the official wording of the governor's offer as it appeared in the Pepin *Courier* ten days later:

PROCLAMATION
$500 REWARD

> Whereas it has been presented to me that on the 10th day of July A.D., 1881, in the county of Pepin, Milton Coleman, Under Sheriff of Dunn county and Charles Coleman, Ex-Sheriff of Pepin county were murdered, and that the murderer or murderers are still at large; and that the ends of justice require that a reward shall be offered by me for their apprehension and conviction. Now, therefore, I, William E. Smith, Governor of the state of Wisconsin, by virtue of the authority vested in me by law, do hereby offer a reward of Five Hundred Dollars, to be paid upon the conviction of said murderer or murderers, to the person or persons who shall apprehend the perpetrator or perpetrators of said crime, and deliver him or them safely to the Sheriff of said county, at the county seat thereof.
>
> In testimony whereof I have here-unto set my hand and caused the [G.S.] Great Seal of the state to be affixed, this twelfth

day of July in the year of our Lord one thousand eight hundred and eighty-one.

(signed)   WILLIAM E. SMITH
By the Governor,
Hans B. Warner, Sec'y of State

Other bounties were added almost immediately. Pepin County offered an amount equal to that of the governor. Henderson County in Illinois already had placed a reward of $200 for the Maxwells for horse theft and larceny before the killings. They telegraphed Sheriff Peterson to emphasize that it was still available. Peterson acknowledged their generosity by tacking the last sentence onto his own announcement of reward:

$500 reward is offered by Pepin county for the arrest of the Williams brothers, who killed Charles and Milton Coleman, at Durand, Wis, Sunday, July 10th, 1881. Henderson county, Ill., offers $200 reward for the same men.

Dunn County was quick to include their disgust with the murderers by putting up an equal share of the reward money:

We the undersigned for and on behalf of the county of Dunn, in the state of Wisconsin, do hereby offer a reward of $500 for the capture of the persons who shot and killed M. A. Coleman, the undersheriff of said county, and his brother, at Durand, Wis. On the 10th day of July, 1881, or $250 for the capture of either of said persons.

SEVER SEVERSON, Sheriff
C. E. FREEMAN, Dist. Atty.

Within days the total reward for the Maxwells' captures stood at $1700. This was a huge sum for the day on the heads of these two desperados. It certainly provided an incentive for the farmers and lumbermen of the region to consider throwing in their lot by joining the posse on the manhunt. For the majority of these hunters, the $1700 jackpot would represent almost an entire year's wages.

William Carson, the gentleman who proposed a benevolent fund for Charlie Coleman's family, had another proposal to offer. He wanted to increase the size of the reward for the Maxwells' capture. He was convinced that a much larger incentive would surely produce much quicker results. He suggested raising the award to the high figure of $5,000 and towards that, he was the first contributor with a pledge of $100. Whether his suggestion was acted upon is not a matter of public record.

During the first day the Maxwells remained hidden in the woods where they'd concealed the buggy. They went down the bank to the Eau Galle several times to bathe their wounds in the river. They were taking no chances on being spotted. It wasn't until that night that they dared to leave. Abandoning the buggy and leaving the horse tethered there to die, they walked the road towards an old schoolhouse at the mouth of Knight's Creek. They met two teams on the road but stepped aside into the brush, letting the teams go on by. But as they approached the schoolhouse, somebody shot at them. A guard had been posted there as a lookout should the boys come that way. The shot missed but sent them running for cover back into the woods. At that point Lon commented that they must have killed somebody in Durand or the law wouldn't be hunting for them.

The shot had come from the gun of Dr. J. R. Branch. He was a picket set up on the road near the schoolhouse. Seeing the two men approaching, and recognizing his quarry, he fired at them. He missed, but frightened the two enough that they remained much more cautious after that about appearing in the open on the roads. His poor aim also left Dr. Branch a target for teasing by his cronies on the hunt.

This telegraph stated that the Maxwell brothers were members of the James and Younger gangs,

This telegram, addressed to His Excellency Honorable W. Smith (the governor) states that the Maxwells were believed early on to be part of the James-Younger Gang. It says: About nine o'clock last night under sheriff Coleman of Dunn County and under sheriff Coleman of Pepin County were shot & killed by two desparadoes (sic) named Ed & Alonzo Williams. They are the James or Younger gang. There is intense excitement and it is thought the state should take some action at once & offer reward.

This livery stable in Durand would have been busy looking after the needs of the horses of the posse during the hunt for the Maxwells. Horses, especially those from beyond Durand, would require feed, stabling and blacksmithing.

For the next couple of days the boys continued to hide in the bush. They had no food until they broke into a nearby milk-house. Ed helped himself to the milk while Lon found some molasses. By now they were weakened from hunger. On Wednesday night they killed a steer then roasted themselves a large piece of a haunch.

While secluded in the woods, they often saw men from the hunting party on the roads looking for them. One time three men on horseback rode so close to them that they were sure they'd be spotted. Raising their Winchester rifles, they were almost ready to fire when Lon said," Don't shoot. We can give them the slip." The posse rode on past and the Maxwells went undetected. According to Ed, who later recognized him, one of the men at whom they were pointing their rifles was Henry Coleman, brother of Charles and Milton.

Immediately following the funerals, Edwin and Henry Coleman had approached their mother saying they felt it their obligation to join the posse. Edwin was a manager of the Bailey Manufacturing Company based out of Knapp. Henry, at 22 years of age, was a crack shot and well known for his prowess at handling a rifle. Their mother fearing for their safety after just losing two boys, was at first reluctant, but understanding how they felt, gave them her blessings to join the searchers.

The posse was on the right track. Knowing some of the Maxwell's habits, they focused on the area around the Eau Galle River bottoms. They were sure that Lon and Ed being so familiar with that territory would feel comfortable hiding out there. The brothers knew the roads and much of the wooded parts of the country. It would be easy for them to elude their pursuers if they remained nearby. But the posse was vigilant and persistent. They began to hear reports of sightings by the locals.

On the day following the shooting in Durand, a Mrs. Pericol and her son, while on their way to Carson and Rand's General Store near Eau Galle about 9 am, saw two men come up the bank from the Eau Galle River. When they saw her, one of the men jumped back into the bushes while the other walked slowly past her. He was carrying two guns. Not knowing about the Durand murders the night before, she mentioned the incident when she reached the store to purchase goods. After describing them, word was hastily sent back to the posse, but by the time they arrived, there was no sign of the Maxwells.

Two days later the horse and buggy was found that they had abandoned in the woods. The horse had been tied to two separate trees with the two halter straps. It was apparent that the horse had not been fed or watered for several days leading the men to believe that the Maxwells were not planning to return to use it. Despite its poor condition when found, the horse later recovered from its ordeal. The buggy, a fairly new one, was a light side-bar single with a top. It had a bullet hole through its black curtain. It had been shot from inside the buggy judging from the powder burns on the cloth. A short distance away was a rubber coat, a harness and a wooden box containing a blacking brush.

That Ed and Alonzo were maintaining a fairly strict routine of sticking to the woods was apparent from the few sightings that were reported of them in the countryside. John Adsit, a farmer out looking for wandering cows about 4 pm on the Saturday after the shootings, saw two men come out of the bush west of his house and follow a fence line. They went back into the woods again where the timber was somewhat thicker behind Jack Allen's home. By the time Doolittle's posse was summoned, the men had vanished. But this was one of the few good clues for a long time that the posse had regarding the whereabouts of the two.

There was some definite concern that the Maxwells would try to return to the Hersey/ Knapp haunts to the north that they knew so well. To make it more difficult for them, the stagecoach route between Menonomie and Brookville was guarded carefully. If they were heading in that direction, it would be tougher for them to make the journey.

About the same time the carcass was found of the steer that the Maxwells had killed, a woman saw them at the Pine Tavern at Eau Galle. She was picking cherries at the time and noticed them in the bush near the tavern. She reported them at the Eau Galle mills, but by the time anyone arrived, they once again had fled down to the river.

The Pine Tavern was a spot with which the Maxwells would be quite familiar.

The Ludington Guard settled in at Maple Springs in the town of Eau Galle. Throughout the entire area pickets were set up around the clock. Nary a tavern or store or public building was without an armed agent keeping vigilance. Even main intersecting roads had guards posted in the bush where they could watch travelers on the roads unobstructed. Early on, Doolittle had established a secondary camp near the mouth of Knights Creek at the old schoolhouse. He placed Dan Harshman in charge of that camp. At a deserted mill on Missouri Creek, another, smaller camp was set up about six miles south of the one on Knights Creek with Captain Frank Kelley in charge. To co-ordinate all of these, a headquarters was established at the Eau Galle mills situated between the others for easier communications. Scouting parties branched out from the camps daily. Later, Sheriff Doolittle and his posse re-established a base camp at Cady Creek north of Eau Galle.

New recruits and volunteers continued to arrive daily offering some assistance. As well, a man named Buffalo Charley joined the team. He too was supposed to be an expert searcher. He was to bring with him a team of bloodhounds trained to ferret out even the most cunning fugitives.

About the same period, a newspaper reporter attached to the *Pioneer Press* in St. Paul showed up to join the searchers. Mr. J. H. Hanson was said to have been with those who hunted and captured the Younger brothers in 1876 near Madelia, Minnesota. Everyone hoped he had brought some good luck to make this hunt as successful. At the very least, it was hoped he could keep his readers accurately informed. Another correspondent from the *Chicago Times* was attached to the Ludington Guards to act as "historian". He provided his readers with a daily "colour commentary" of the manhunt.

These weren't the only media men interested in following the Maxwell story. An artist, Jacob Miller, accompanied the search as well hoping to get a first-hand portrait sitting by Ed and Lon. While with the hunters, he drew some sketches of the physical aspects of the chase. As subjects for his artistry he chose to sketch the scene of the murders, the old schoolhouse at Knight's Creek, Bill Thompson's house where the Maxwells had reportedly visited frequently, and the spot where the horse and buggy had been abandoned and found. Whether Miller ever published any of his drawings or sold any privately is not known. His pictures would be interesting because the searchers' camps were soon to be disbanded. Because of the rarity of cameras in that era, there were no photographs of the chase.

The wounds both Ed and Lon had suffered from the Coleman's shotgun blasts gave them trouble. In a few days they festered and began to show signs of infection. Their arms were badly swollen and Lon's especially became bad. For a while there was a fear it might have to be amputated because of the risk of the infection worsening. They continued to bathe their wounds and gradually the infections cleared, but they were both left with scars.

Sightings were infrequent but even when they occurred they rarely provided enough time for the posse to move in for the capture. Almost a week after the killings a young man saw the Maxwells about 40 rods away from Perry Treat's saloon at Eau Galle. Terrified, he did not report the incident until the next morning despite the fact that there was a posse member stationed close by.

The next day two boys had a brief conversation with the Maxwell brothers. The Maxwells inquired of the boys how many men were in the posse. They also wanted to know if the sheriff had recently been up that road. Then one of the two measured the tracks in the road and said that the sheriff had indeed gone by. The incident, though minor, at least illustrated the frustration the Maxwells were beginning to feel.

Captain Kelley located a faint trail near Bill Thompson's place. He found traces of blood and evidence of the Maxwells having dressed their wounds and rested. For whatever reasons, he discovered that one of them was wearing a boot on one foot and a moccasin on the other. Later it was learned that Ed had twisted an ankle and sought relief using a moccasin on the sore foot.

The hunt itself was not without incident. One of the posse members, a fellow named Kelley Nott, managed to shoot himself in the shoulder with his own rifle. It was Kelley's sister, Rosa, to whom Milt Coleman was engaged to be married. With some others, Kelley had done some target shooting about six miles from town. After they were finished, he reloaded his carbine for the search and placed it beside him in the wagon. While driving his team ahead, the rough road caused the gun to discharge hitting him in the shoulder and fracturing the bone. Gunshot wounds were common enough then that the *Dunn County News* brushed off the incident saying, "Fortunately, the wound did not prove to be serious…"

Nott wasn't the only casualty. About the third week of the hunt, seven of the searchers from Doolittle's party traveling in a wagon were thrown from their vehicle when it tipped on a rough road. One gentleman from Knapp, J. Q. Bailey, seriously injured his back and had to be returned to his home. The others apparently suffered no lasting injuries.

The thought that the Maxwells could be in their neighbourhoods had everyone on edge. People took no chances but suspected anyone who was a stranger. Having not one, but two murderers on the loose created a very uneasy tension. The citizens of Hersey and Knapp were especially nervous because theirs was an area that had not only been frequented in the past by the "Williams" brothers as they were known around there, but Ed and Lon had worked and lived in that vicinity. Some people living there were known to be still friendly towards them. It was almost expected that eventually they would make their way back that far north again to reach their familiar habitats.

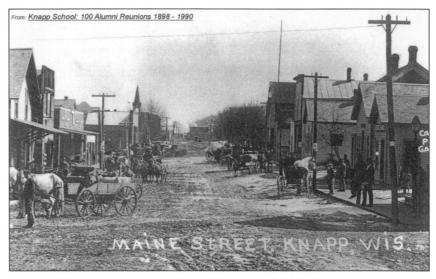

From: *Knapp School: 100 Alumni Reunions 1898 - 1990*

MAINE STREET, KNAPP, WIS.

1900 - Main Street of Knapp, Wisconsin

Exactly two weeks after the killings, on Sunday July 24th, David McCullough spotted a man sleeping in one of his hayfields on a farm about ten miles from the community of Knapp. A storm had just passed through the area, and the man, probably seeking shelter from the storm, had fallen asleep under a haycock. McCullough, thinking the man might be one of the "Williams" brothers, hastily raced into Knapp to rouse the authorities there. To illustrate the nervousness area people were feeling, or perhaps inspired by the promise of a $1700 reward, forty-seven fully armed men in short order surround-ed McCullough's hayfield. They were led by Captain McMullen of that same village. Hollering into the field towards the haycock, they demanded that the interloper surrender. After not hearing any re-sponse, they began cautiously to cross the field towards the haycock where the man had been hiding.

On a signal, they charged the haycock pulling it apart assuming the culprit had buried himself deeper in the mound, but they were wrong. It was empty. Knowing he couldn't have gone far, the stalwart troop of volunteers performed another rapid raid on a clump of willows at the field's edge. This time they met with success. Flushing out their prey, they seized on the man who immediately threw up his arms in the air and surrendered when he sensed how futile it would be to try to flee.

As the man stood completely encircled by dozens of rifles all pointed directly at him, Captain McMullen approached the fellow pulling off his hat for a better look at his face But another disappointment awaited the band from Knapp. The man was not either of the Maxwells. He was simply a wandering tramp in the area looking to escape the bad weather. As one last verification, O. S. Hurlburt came forward to demand of the man that he remove his boots. By now the poor vagrant was overwhelmed with fear and immediately did as he was instructed. Fortunately for him, the man had all ten toes intact. And no other physical feature resembled either Ed or Alonzo. It turned out that the man was in the neighbourhood working earlier for a Mr. Cochrane near Lucas. Now looking for another harvesting job, he was wandering the area. The tramp was released with nothing more than a good fright, and the Knapp posse returned home having lost nothing but time.

After more than two full weeks of intense searching without any reliable sightings in the last five or six days, the toll on the searchers was becoming evident. Over-tired from long hours on the ground or in the saddle, coupled with little comfortable sleep, less-than-nutritious food and the humidity of the mid-summer air, the posse members began to feel ill and exhausted. Even Edwin Coleman, the older surviving brother of Milt and Charlie, was reported to have been forced to return from the hunt by July 27th. Said to be unfit for continued duty, he went to stay at the home of his mother while he recuperated. No doubt there were many others in similar physical condition before the third full week expired.

By the following week though, the trail was beginning to grow cold. What the posse didn't know was that the Maxwell boys had begun heading to the Mississippi so they could start back south. They moved only at night to avoid easy detection or being recognized. They passed through Plum City and continued southwest until reaching the Mississippi River in the vicinity of Maiden Rock. There they stole a boat to cross Lake Pepin over to the Minnesota shore. The full knowledge of what transpired in Durand was known to them only after they read a newspaper in Minnesota. After that, they were even more cautious about being seen.

For the next several weeks they slept by day and travelled by night. They obtained food and supplies by sneaking into houses and stealing what they could. Sometimes if the pickings were lean, they went several days without anything to eat.

The frustration of the searchers was beginning to show. Then too, it was well into haying and harvest season. Most of the searchers were rural people who relied on bringing in a crop in order to have a good winter. Many had to drift off home to get the farm work finished. They felt they had to temporarily set aside the chase for the elusive Maxwells because of pressing demands from the homefront.

Adding to the difficulty of locating the killers was the mis-information regarding their appearances. Ed was described as being fully three inches taller than his five feet, three inches height, having blue eyes instead of dark brown eyes, and weighing twenty pounds more than his real weight of 140 pounds. He was accurately said to be wearing a moustache and goatee, but a second description reported he had only a short, black moustache.

Courtesy Pepin County Historical Society

This fine buggy standing outside a photography shop in Durand might
be in front of Bachelder's Gallery. Bachelder advertised in the Courier
that he had "photographs of the notorious Williams brothers"for sale.

Alonzo was described having auburn hair instead of light brown.
The rest of his portrayal though was fairly accurate. He was said to
be not as heavy as Ed, and to have a light moustache and brown eyes.
Another description said he had "no whiskers unless artificial". He
was said to have sharper features and to weigh more than his older
brother.

The confusion is easy to understand by reading the wordings
posted by two newspapers only one week apart:

Detailed portrayal of the Maxwells in *The News* in Menonomie,
July 16, 1881:

> Ed. Williams, alias "Maxwell", is about 30 to 35 years old, dark
> complexion, dark blue eyes, black hair, generally wears a goatee,
> is about 5 feet 6 inches in height and weighs about 155 pounds,
> well built, good looking, and wears a gold watch and chain. Alonzo
> Williams, alias "Maxwell", is about 25 to 30 years old, fair com-
> plexion, brown hair, and moustache and goatee, keen dark gray
> eyes, light built, sharp features, about 5 feet 8 or 9 inches in height,
> weight between 140 and 150 pounds.

An interesting comparison can be made with the description given in the Pepin *Courier* of July 22:

Description — Edward is rather heavy set, broad across the shoulders, stout, well-built, black hair, dark complexion, had short black moustache, very sharp dark blue eyes, weight about 140 lbs., hight (sic) about 5 ft. 7 inches, about 30 years of age. Lon is not so heavy set, auburn hair, dark brown eyes, fair complexion, no whiskers unless artificial, weight about 150 lbs., about 5ft 10 inches in hight (sic) rather sharper features than the other, about 25 years old, has lost the 2nd toe on his right foot, both are supposed to be wounded with shot. They carry Winchester rifles.

Telegraph any information to.
MILETUS KNIGHT.
Under Sheriff, Pepin Co. Wis.
Durand, Wis.

In an interesting turnabout, one report said that the Williams brothers also use the alias "Maxwell". One other account suggested that they had a brother still living at Macomb, Illinois. That too was inaccurate as their brothers had moved to Nebraska with their parents years before.

To suggest that life was much different in the 1880's than today would be a gross understatement. So much of every facet of our lives has altered drastically and significantly from that era. Everything is different from the way we work, the foods we eat, the type of occupations we engage in, the clothing we wear, the type of transportation we use, and the leisure activities we enjoy. Almost nothing escaped significant change over the decades.

This included the places where people lived. Most of the country of the 1880's was an agrarian society. Farming was the mainstay for folks' livelihoods and people did not often venture very far. They were required to be there to nurture what was grown on the land. Communities were relatively close to each other. They were smallish, but they were within the distance one could ride by horse or buggy to get there within an hour or two. And they often depended on one of three main modes of transportation: horseback (or horse-drawn vehicle such as a sleigh, wagon or buggy), railway or riverboat. Without one or more of these, no town or village would survive for very long. Conversely, the more of these three means that would provide access, the stronger the chances of that community's survival.

The rivers allowed for easy delivery of timber to be brought down-stream. Huge log rafts were often a mile long. Waterpower from the river permitted the growth of grist mills with water-wheels to grind the grain. No community even today survives without a viable source of potable water for drinking and cleaning. But a good waterway can also transport people in the commercial or personal comings and goings. The docks often were a haven of entertainment and a meeting place, a central agora for the river community.

Courtesy P.M. O'Brien from *Spring Brook Saga*

One of the several steamboats that plied the
Chippewa River in the 1880's.

What didn't arrive easily by waterway could be delivered by rail. Freight cars were the money-makers for the rail-lines. Goods that were necessary for daily life or for the business of commerce were transported in by rail. And equally important was the ability to export out of town any commodities to sell. Commuting by train was far more frequent then. More people traveled by rail, especially if the distances they were going were long. Not that the train cars were comfortable. They weren't. A trip by rail always exposed the traveller to the risk of cinders in the eye or clothes dirtied by smoke. But the trains were available. Access was the key. Rail lines were plentiful and one could travel within range of almost anywhere by coach back then. Towns grew or died depending on their relationship to the railroad. More than a few of today's ghost towns fell victim to the re-routing of rail lines which left them bereft of service. The concept is not unlike today's smaller towns being by-passed by our national super-highways.

Small hamlets abounded during the early days. Often five to ten miles apart, they serviced mainly the agrarian society immediately around them. One could usually count on a few amenities in each community; a hotel or two, several more taverns, a livery stable where the transport or pack animals would be also bedded and fed, and a general store or emporium. Depending on the size of the community, there might also be a doctor, a blacksmith, post-office, school, churches of a few denominations, barber, pharmacist, dressmaker, cooper, tailor or wagon-maker. These small villages were the foundation of the rural way of life.

Such a place was the town of Ella, Wisconsin in the 1880's. Founded in 1872, Ella was fortunate to be served by all three transportation links. Located on the Chippewa River about ten miles south of Durand, it was visited almost daily by the paddle-wheeler "Red Wing" as it plied the Chippewa. A railroad at that time wound between Wabasha and Durand. For fifteen cents passengers could make the journey through some rather interesting scenery. Part of that scenery was the little village of Ella where the train stopped to take on and discharge passengers. Because of the agriculture in the region, there were many roads throughout the farming areas. Blessed with access by all three travel modes, Ella seemed to be in an enviable situation for growth.

The little village prospered. Like so many riverbank towns, only part of the town's buildings could be built along the water. The terrain was such that the rest of the town was built on higher ground away from the water leaving Ella with an "uptown" and a "downtown" section. But the town sprawled to meet the growth it was experiencing. In an ideal location such as it had, success continued for Ella for some time.

There was an interesting idiosyncrasy to the town of Ella. It eventually acquired three different names. By road, it was called Ella; by river it was known as Shoo Fly; by railroad it was Maxville. (Today this last name is the one by which it continues to be identified on road maps and atlases.)

Eventually though, the town was subjected to some fluctuations over which it had no control. Two very significant situations impacted on the town. The first was the level of the Chippewa River began to drop consistently over the years.

The Ella Hotel circa 1905

This reduced the log flow down-river to the sawmills which eventually went out of business or changed venues when they could no longer operate with the cheap water power. The mills suffered the same loss of power and were forced to look elsewhere for more efficient power. The dropping of the water levels also curtailed the transport of the steamboats and paddle-wheelers. That, of course, meant no more passengers, no more tourists, no more flow of money into the pretty little town that depended so heavily on the river traffic.

The second change that helped bring about the demise of Ella was the closure of the railroad. No longer economically sound, the rail-line was retired. That meant another source of income lost to the town. Goods would no longer arrive or leave by train resulting in rising costs. Except for wagons and buggies on the land roads the ability to move commodities in or out conveniently all but dried up. By then Ella was on its way to becoming a Wisconsin ghost town.

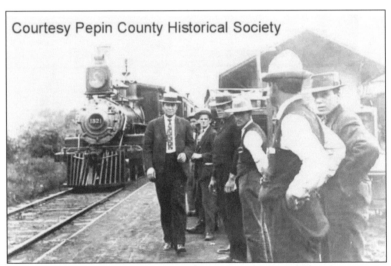

Courtesy Pepin County Historical Society

Although some smaller communities lost their rail service for geographical and fiscal reasons, other towns reflected growth as the railroads expanded their lines into them. The Durand depot shown above did not come about until July 1882. Passenger trains, as well as freight cars were soon scheduled.

Small communities such as Ella were ideal for the Maxwells. Lon and Ed were able to move in and out quietly, unobtrusively, acquire by hook or by crook the supplies they needed, and leave, knowing that probably few people would recognize them. Ella was much like the other vil-

lages the Maxwells frequented. Places like Plum City, Maiden Rock, Moziers Landing, Kampsville, Eau Galle, Hersey and Pearl, despite being in different states, shared the commonality of being similar in make-up; they were small, anonymous and accessible. They served the Maxwells perfectly to remain obscured from the public eye.

The news of the murders and the manhunt for the Maxwells made the newspapers throughout several states. The only other story that took precedence over this one was the attempted assassination of President Garfield by his assailant, Charles J. Guiteau on July 2ⁿᵈ. But one report in particular is worth mentioning for the simplicity of its ironic understatement. The *Stillwater Messenger* of July 16, 1881 carried the following comment:

The Maxwell brothers, two outlaws who murdered the Coleman brothers at Durand, Wis., a few days ago, are being hunted down and will probably be captured. They will die with their boots on.

The writer could hardly have guessed to what extent his prophecy would ring true.

The KENTUCKY STORY

THE EFFORT TO CAPTURE the Maxwells and put them behind Joliet's prison bars not only made people feel safer, it provided them with something other than the weather to talk about, or President Garfield's plight to read. The newspapers of the day seized on the Maxwell story and capitalized on a readership hungry to learn more about their exploits.

One thing about a good journalist, when he's onto an absorbing story, he can be very persistent. That means checking and double-checking, and most importantly of all, looking for the different angles from which the story can be told. It's not enough to just get out the facts. A riveting story has to take on a life of its own. It has to stand alone as the most intriguing, most provocative piece of information that the reader could get into his hands.

To achieve that sense of fascination for his audience, the good journalist will ferret out everything pertinent to the story that he can find. But the truly great journalist will keep digging; will look under all the rugs, open all the cupboards to know what's behind every door. Then look for more.

A reporter with the *Chicago Herald* went probing for some background information on the Maxwell boys. Wanting to present a closer perspective of just what these lads had been engaged in during their past, he interviewed an acquaintance of theirs who was willing to talk and shed some light on the nature of their "work", but who remained unnamed for reasons that will become obvious. He was described though as a "well-known sporting man".

Asked if he knew the Maxwells, he said, "Yes, I knew them intimately."

He went on to tell how he had become acquainted with these ruffians. "I met Lon Maxwell in a saloon one night. There was a row against him. I don't like to see a dozen men against one, so stepped up beside him and took his part. Afterwards I met his brother Ed, and we became fast friends."

When asked about the Maxwells' means of making a living, the 'sport' said they were horse dealers. Asked if he meant horse thieves, he said it was pretty much the same thing anyway. He acknowledged that he was in the same line of work, but if the Maxwells wanted a horse they couldn't buy, they'd just steal it.

The confederate said though, that until he met the Maxwell brothers, he had never stolen a horse. Sounding much like a modern-day used-car salesman, he admitted to being guilty of passing off a lesser quality animal as being better than it was, but denied any thievery involved in his business until then.

"One day", he said, "Lon Maxwell came to me and said he and Ed were going over into Kentucky to look at some horses and asked me to go with them. That was my first and last horse stealing expedition. My experience then convinced me that I was not cut out for a successful horse thief."

He claimed that at the outset he had no idea what they were going to do. When the boys let him in on their scheme, he wanted to back out, but they taunted him into remaining with them. They visited farms in the area looking out for the best horse-flesh. They let on that they had come from Missouri and that money was no object.

Eventually they found what they were looking for. A black stallion and two bay geldings caught their fancy. According to the 'sport', they were worth $1000 each if they were worth a cent. The trick was to make an escape with them. They asked the owners to saddle and bridle the three horses under the guise of riding them to try them for their merits. "We rode off together, and the owner never saw hide or hair of them again."

But the plan didn't go as smoothly as they had hoped. After realizing he had been duped, the owner organized a posse in an attempt to regain his valuable steeds.

"We dodged around for a week, and still they kept after us. One morning just about day-break they came up to a farm where we were eating breakfast. A little boy warned us of their approach, and we had just got out by the back door and reached the stable when they drove up to the front door. We knew we were in for a fight, our horses were tied, but we didn't want it to take place right there."

They rode away as rapidly as possible with the posse in hot pursuit. In true characteristic Maxwell style, they headed for a wooded area in the hills about two miles in the distance. Once there, they dove for the trees as a "shower of bullets" pelted the tree branches around them. The posse was estimated to be about a dozen in number.

The Maxwells, unfamiliar with the area, dismounted as soon as they were in the shelter of the thicker bush. Lon grabbed the three horses by the reins and tethered them behind, out of danger in a ravine while Ed and their new cohort focused on the posse.

What he went on to describe was a classic wild-west style shoot-out. "For a few minutes the firing was pretty brisk," he said, "and then our pursuers retired out of pistol shot carrying with them four of their number who were killed or disabled. Neither Lon or Ed were hit, but it seemed to me that most every bullet found its lodging place in my carcass. My clothes were all torn to pieces and I had six or eight wounds. They were mere scratches however…"

While the sheriff's posse was tending to their casualties, the Maxwells slipped back to their horses and rode out the back way without being noticed. He admitted that the stolen horses were sold for good prices, but insisted that was his last episode of horse thievery.

"I broke with the Maxwells boys after that, and have never seen them since."

Asked if he thought the Maxwells would be captured and taken alive for the Durand shootings, he said, "No, I don't. They have been at large for three weeks and they know that entire country as well as you do the alphabet. At any rate, they will never allow themselves to be taken alive, and it will cost many lives to kill them. According to all reports, they are armed with Winchester rifles and six-shooters, and have plenty of ammunition. Under the circumstances, I wouldn't like to try conclusions with them, even if I had fifty men at my back."

BUFFALO CHARLEY

A TRACKER, REPUTEDLY AN expert government scout, arrived at the Cady base camp at Maple Springs on July 28th. Charles Lewis, known better as "Buffalo Charley", was hailed as an Indian scout who had reportedly performed under General George Custer of Little Big Horn fame. It was also believed that he served under General Nelson Miles, who had achieved early recognition during the Indian Wars and later during countless Civil War battles. Buffalo Charley, by association, arrived with impressive credentials to the Maxwell manhunt.

Besides bringing his reputation and his personage to the chase, he was said to be arriving with his pack of thirty bloodhounds that would surely ferret out the desperados once they got on the scent. The claim too, was that he would be accompanied by six or eight other tracking scouts to assist him.

Buffalo Charley did make his appearance, but it didn't take long for the old veterans on the hunt to recognize him as a complete fraud. Arriving alone with neither additional scouts nor any bloodhounds, the posse members soon realized that Charley wasn't what he claimed to be. Within days they had renamed him "Bogus Charley". Captain Doolittle assigned him to one of the hunting parties but the man was monitored carefully for signs of incompetence. It was evident that he knew little of woodsmanship or tracking. He was far more interested in the contents of the mess tent than the trail he was to be following.

When the good sheriff was satisfied that Charley really was a fraud, Doolittle had him arrested and taken to jail in Menonomie. It was generally understood that he would be far less a nuisance there than in the woods. But some of the posse members couldn't resist the temptation to rattle Charley a bit by suggesting that he might deserve having his neck stretched.

Little information was known about him except that he had a German background and had lived at New Ulm back around the time of the Indian Massacre of 1862. He claimed that he was the only member of his family to escape. It turned out that Charley was not without a criminal past. He had worked in a hotel in Pewaukee until June. On July 25th he was released from a thirty-day term in jail at La Crosse for breaking into a freight car there. By the time he managed to get north to Lake City, he learned of the hunt for the "Williams" brothers. Thinking this an easy meal-ticket for a while, he passed himself off as a tracking scout. It seems his best tracks all led to the food larder. In the end, all he located was more trouble for himself.

WIND-DOWN OF THE WISCONSIN HUNT

By late July it was becoming apparent that the hunt was not going to be successful. The Maxwells, it seemed, had slipped through the net cast around the Eau Galle area. The search in that vicinity was called off as there had not been a reliable report of sighting them for some time.

Doolittle's posse was still camped on Cady Creek east of Eau Galle and north of Durand. At Maple Springs, slightly to the west, the Ludington Guard had its headquarters. A general meeting of the minds from both camps agreed that remaining on the search in that area with such intensity was beginning to grow futile. The decision was made to order the Guard back to Menonomie. They returned Sunday, July 31, exactly three weeks after the Colemans had been gunned down. Doolittle and his party remained another four days, but on the following Thursday the weary posse members broke camp and returned to their homes as well. Officially the hunt would continue until the Maxwells were captured, but for now the search would be a matter of maintaining a vigil.

The next day, August 5th, the *Pepin County Courier* noted that the outlaws no doubt had some "assistants in the woods" who were helping them out of "sheer cussedness". Since the friends were known, they would be dealt with "in proper time".

This was not the first time such a suggestion had been made in the press. The resulting "guilt by association" prompted Edward Wolf to write a letter to the editor which appeared in its August 5th edition of the *Hudson Star and Times*. Ed Wolf decried any assistance by himself or his brothers to the Maxwells, known to him as the Williams:

> "The reason why people have our names connected with the Williamses is that we have been acquainted with them so long, and then Lon boarded a spell at my house when he first came to the town. I never cared for his company, but I knew it was better to have his good will than his ill."

Ed Wolf's letter threw an interesting light upon the deportment of the Maxwells in Hersey and on an incident there:

> "Lon ... behaved like a gentleman all the time he was here until his brother Ed came. They were here about three months when they drove Sheriff Kelly off... they simply pointed a revolver at him and his partner and told them to get, which they did, and staid (sic) at the depot till train time, while the Williams boys shouldered their Winchesters and a little sack with provisions and coolly walked out of town. All these things are highly embellished by your correspondent. The Williams never went around this town brandishing firearms and intimidating all the inhabitants as reported in the *Pioneer Press.*

While Ed Wolf's denial was rather lengthy and tactfully worded to suggest that they were not fully in sympathy with Ed and Alonzo, he never actually came right out and said that they did not give the Maxwells any provisions.

The hunt for the killers was further hampered by poor communication and mis-information that was circulated. Some of it, such as wrong sightings or exaggerated circumstances, was frustrating. Often it required searchers to go well out the way to check out phantom facts. Some might have been almost humorous if it weren't for the maliciousness of the content. For example, it was reported that Sheriff Doolittle and two posse members had been killed by the Maxwells in the woods near Eau Galle. That rumour originated apparently in Lake City, Minnesota. In an effort to ensure accuracy, the Sheriff sent a dispatch to the *St. Paul Pioneer Press* informing that newspaper that the report of his death was not truthful at all. Somewhat reminiscent of Mark Twain's comment, "The reports of my death are greatly exaggerated", the message was the same, but Twain put it more eloquently than did the exasperated Doolittle.

On another sour note, Sheriff Severson in Menonomie had to try to recover some equipment loaned out to some of the searchers during the Maxwell hunt. His displeasure can be heard in the sarcasm of his announcement:

> All parties who were furnished with the saddles and carbines belonging to the Ludington Guard, during the hunt for the Williams desperados, and have neglected to return them are hereby notified to do so without delay. They should have been returned long ago. I should have sent for them before this, but for the reason that I thought the parties men of honor who would bring them back without making me unnecessary trouble and expense.
>
> SEVER SEVENSON,
> Sheriff, Dunn County

Shortly after Doolittle's posse disbanded, Sheriff Anderson returned to Illinois on the ferry *Gem City*. He took with him the horse which had been stolen by the Maxwells back on May the 30th and which Sheriff Miletus Knight had found secreted at Mrs. Senz' place. Shortly after the horse was stolen, Anderson had sent out post cards to as many law agencies as he could, notifying sheriffs of the Maxwells' crimes and the reward offered. It was as a result of these cards that Knight located the horses and that the Colemans knew of the outlaws.

On his way back to Illinois, Anderson learned that two men resembling the fugitives had been seen on the river in a skiff posing as trappers. They were armed with both rifles and revolvers. Sheriff Anderson believed from the information he was given that Ed and Alonzo may be making their way back to the part of the country with which they again would be both familiar and comfortable.

Besides being an inveterate lawman, Sheriff Anderson was also a great humanitarian. On learning that Charlie Coleman left his widow and family in dire financial straits, he took the initiative back in Illinois to create a benevolent fund for the survivors. The people of Illinois demonstrated their generosity quickly. In its early inception, the list of donors was topped by a single contribution of $100 and the collection effort showed the goodwill of the Illinois people.

For the time being there was no other progress in the manhunt. The Maxwells virtually drifted into a temporary obscurity.

JOHN LAMMY and the BATTLE of FOX CREEK

By SEPTEMBER THE SEARCH for the Maxwell boys in Wisconsin was all but over. Officially they were still being hunted, but in reality the searchers knew they'd have to await a major break in the case. Newspapers reported that the sheriff and his men were keeping a lookout for them. The authorities realized Ed and Alonzo had escaped through their net and it was going to be a matter of time waiting to see where they'd resurface.

This was an elusive pair of outlaws. Years of practice had taught them to travel by night, hide by day. Their only daylight travel would be at a distance from other people, making positive identification almost impossible. On the Mississippi River for instance, two men travelling in a skiff would seem so natural that hardly anyone would pay attention to them. Besides, nobody would likely get close enough to see just who they were. Dressed as hunters or loggers, they'd blend perfectly into the river mosaic.

Moving downriver in a stolen skiff, Ed and Alonzo established a base for themselves on the Mississippi at Mozier Island. From there they conducted raids on local farmhouses stealing what foodstuffs they could to furnish themselves with meals. Frequently they would avail themselves of a farmer's hospitality to stay for a meal. Ed and Alonzo were both quite articulate and could be very charming. Although ruthless at their burglary, they would also extend warmth to those who offered them friendship.

That two armed strangers would present themselves at a farmhouse requesting a meal or lodging, was not uncommon in that era. It was the accepted norm for anyone making their way across country to entreat hospitality this way. Hotels or taverns were often few and far between. (The word "restaurant" hadn't even been put to use yet.) Besides, they cost money that most vagrants couldn't afford. Many rural areas had no lodging facilities for miles in any direction, but wayfarers were still plentiful. The practice of petitioning a night's stay or a meal was a time-honoured means that had practical benefits for both parties. A comfortable night's sleep or refreshing meal at a farmhouse fulfilled the needs of the traveller. Those who could afford a small payment found it welcomed by rural folks who had few alternatives to bringing in extra cash. Those who could not pay would most often pay "in kind" by working it off at the woodpile or hay-field. "Work for food" was a concept understood well over a hundred years ago.

Strangers arrived not only weary and hungry, but also full of information from other parts of the country. Passing through other areas as they did, they brought with them news from the places they'd been, along with descriptive accounts of adventures encountered along the way. In an age of slower communication and fewer types of entertainment, farmers and their entire families relished the stories told by the visitors. Scheduled work would be set aside to make time to listen to the tales of the wanderers as they related anecdotes or embellished the accounts picked up along the way. It was an opportunity to learn the news and to be entertained.

The fact that many wanderers were carrying firearms was not undue cause for concern. The war was barely 15 years past and many had not yet given up their personal insecurity. Many men considered a holster and sidearm as a wardrobe accessory. In the wild and wooly west, almost everyone wore revolvers or carried rifles in their scabbards. Of those living closer to the Mississippi, some retained their firepower for protection; for others it was used for their livelihood.

Hunters and trappers carried rifles and pistols as part of their equipment. Back then, the sight of a couple of men with firearms elicited no particular excitement on a fall day in deer country.

Without them being aware of it, the Maxwell boys had been spotted by a sheriff's deputy near Pearl on the Illinois River in Pike County. The deputy, George W. Roberts, was out hunting squirrels with his young son when he met two men in the woods resting on a log. Thinking it might be the murderers from photographs he had seen, he approached them and struck up a conversation. As hunters will, they compared notes about their respective rifles. Roberts told the one carrying a carbine that the rifle was a beauty and asked if he might handle it. Maxwell agreed, but possibly as a safety precaution, took Roberts' gun in exchange. Roberts noticed how the second man, leaning against a tree, held one arm behind his back on his hip pocket, constantly watching him.

The rifle was a Winchester, the same type that they had been reported to be using. Convinced by now that these two men really were the Maxwells, Roberts alerted his department superiors.

Sheriff E.W. Blades received Roberts' telegram the next morning. Blades, now armed with a warrant for the two men, set out by 10 am with a posse. Before leaving though, Blades also telegraphed to Pittsfield for additional backup, and made a point of notifying other departments in the area. In all probability, the outlaws were in the Pearl area on a raid as it was about 23 miles from their lair near the Mozier neighbourhood. But now the authorities knew roughly in what part of the country to concentrate their search.

Once in the vicinity of Pearl, the posse began making inquiries about the two strangers. It was found that on that morning they had breakfast at Peter Wicket's house near the place where Roberts had found them. Wicket pointed the direction in which the men had left, leading Blades to discover that the two had lunch at Samuel Braun's home. The Braun family, after seeing the photos carried by Sheriff Blades of the Maxwells, positively identified them as the same two who had partaken the noon meal with them.

As it was obvious that the Maxwells were heading west, Blades divided his force into two bands and split up, taking different roads. At five in the afternoon they re-joined, having had no luck on either road. Determining that the outlaws had left the main thoroughfares and had taken a secondary road, they found that the boys had gone along a ravine. The posse followed a similar route and came out near Belleview north of Mozier Landing. By now it was getting dark so the search was discontinued for the night.

The next morning Blades sent a horseman with a message to Sheriff Lammy of Hardin in Calhoun County informing him that the desperados were in the region and requested his assistance. Lammy had known for a couple of weeks of the presence of the outlaws and had previously tried to track them to no avail. Notified now by the messenger of the Maxwells being near his jurisdiction, Lammy, together with a posse consisting of John Churchman, Frank McNabb, L.M. Tevis and Joe Bizaillion, set out to join forces with Sheriff Blades. Before leaving, he was warned of the heavy danger involved in dealing with those murderers. He is quoted as having said, "The people of this county have repeatedly elected me to the office, and it is as little as I can do to risk my life for them."

Lammy's squad reached Belleview, and together with Sheriff's Blades' men, they combed the Belleview area until 2 pm without success. The only clues were that the two Maxwells had been refused breakfast at two houses that morning. Gottlieb Quiller probably didn't like the looks of two heavily armed men that early in the day. The name of the second household has been forgotten. The other clue was that they had passed John Crosby's farmhouse earlier in the forenoon. The two sheriffs' companies split up, Lammy going southeast and Blades traveling northeast. Making a complete circuit, they met at the farm of H. Nevis where they retired for the night.

On Sunday, September 25th, Ed and Lon had breakfast two miles north of Mozier Landing at the Barnes' home. After their morning meal they headed south. A few hours later they availed themselves of lunch at the home of a Mrs. Beach at Fox Creek. During the meal Mrs. Beach noticed that the men seemed wary and that every once in a while one of them would go to the door and look outside and that they kept careful watch on their guns. At the time, she didn't think anything untoward of this behavior. They offered to pay the lady for her kindness, but times being what they were, she refused payment satisfied that she had helped someone in need with her generosity. Ed, however, slipped young nine-year-old Amy Beach a half-dollar coin before he and Lon continued on.

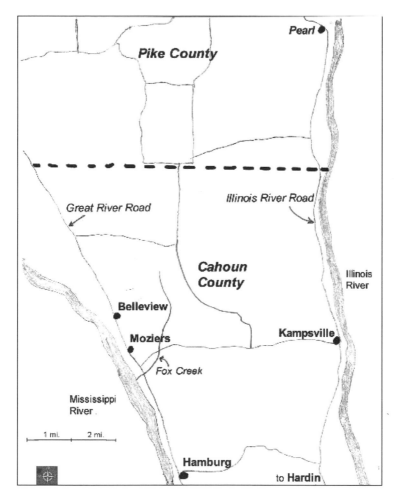

The events of the minutes after leaving the Beach house are probably best described by John Churchman in a sworn statement published in the *Calhoun Herald*. Paragraphing has been repaired for the sake of readability but most spelling and punctuation have been left as it appeared in his original text:

"The combined law forces of Calhoun and Pike Counties were grouped at Lawrence Roth's farm about one-quarter mile from Bay, Illinois. They had gotten word that the Maxwell brothers – two desperate outlaws, were cutting through Calhoun County, moving south. Pike County Sheriff E.W. Blades was riding in a spring wagon with Henry Darr of Crooked Creek and had three deputies on horses. Blades decided to take his men and look in the area of north and west Panther Creek for the outlaws – Deadly killers.

Sheriff Lammy had me (Churchman) to post a lookout for the outlaws at Bay. When I got back to the Roth farm, Lammy, with deputies Frank McNabb, Jim Hayes and G.W. Roberts were about to mount their horses and ride to the Barnes place to look for the outlaws when someone looked south across Roth's field and saw a man with a gun on his shoulder going down Fox Creek.

In his deposition, John Churchman never makes clear just which bandit they confront first. According to Sheriff Blades who would have been informed by his two posse members, Hayes and Roberts who were there, it was Alonzo whom they confronted first carrying the rifle. This would make sense since Lon was more comfortable, not to mention very accurate, with a long gun. Nor was he shy about being first into the shooting. That had been the case in Durand against the Colemans.

What we didn't know was that the other outlaw was walking a few yards ahead – out of view. I (Churchman) had a fast pony, and I rode straight for the creek to cut the fellow off and find out who he was.

John Lammy rode with me, and when I rode into the creek, Lammy turned down the road and was riding abreast of me along side the creek.

Like many small creeks and streams, Fox Creek did not always contain water. In the late summer and fall, it may not have had any at all. That the Maxwells were walking in the creek bed suggests that it was fairly dry. Churchman and McNabb rode the creek on their horses. Churchman never referred to there being any water, seeing any wet footprints or hearing movement in water. It was probably mostly dry.

Frank McNabb rode to the end of Roth's field and into the creek. Frank and I were now riding slowly towards each other. I looked up ahead and saw Frank and shouted to him saying, "Did you see anything of that fellow?" and he answered, "No."

I stopped my horse, McNabb still riding towards me, and I spoke again and said, "Where the devil do you suppose that man has gone to?"

At that moment Frank and I saw the outlaw sitting on a log, behind a tree from me. Frank, by this time had ridden up within twenty yards of him, thinking he could get by to where I was and get our crowd together.

Suddenly the outlaw jumped up, leveled his gun on McNabb, and ordered him to get down off his horse and come up to him or he'd blow his brains out if he didn't. I immediately jumped off my pony and hitched it, and I shouted to Frank not to do it but to "shoot the son of a bitch".

Fearing that Maxwell would shoot Frank, I pulled my pistol and fired at the outlaw's head. The latter turned and fired at me. Frank took advantage of this interval and jumped for cover behind a tree and fired at Maxwell.

At the same time Maxwell gave a loud whistle and the other outlaw came from the slope to the creek firing a handgun. The fight became general. Before this, Jim Hayes and G.W. Roberts, who had double barrel-shotguns, had come down within about 60 yards of the fighting. I (Churchman) yelled for the shotguns to come up, as we had the Maxwells. But Hayes and Roberts hid under the creek bank and did not use their shotguns which were loaded for the occasion.

John Lammy started firing his revolver from the road side of the creek and Frank returned the outlaws' fire from where he had taken cover. I was hit by a bullet from the big rifle and another bullet hit and broke my pistol. Frank McNabb was wounded and no longer shooting.

Churchman did not detail his injury in this report, but he was wounded in the fleshy part of his left leg above the knee. This shot would have been fired by Alonzo who was the outlaw with the big bore rifle. McNabb was shot in his right shoulder. That effectively put an end to McNabb's fighting.

> The outlaws started coming my way. I was wounded and my gun broken so I made for Sheriff Lammy. As I ran past John Lammy I said to him, "John, get away from here quick or you will be killed in a second."
>
> Lammy made no reply but came along with me and fired his gun. I was then a few steps ahead of him making for a tree. I reached the tree first. Lammy came running for the tree with his head half turned, looking back, when Maxwell came out in plain view in the road and shot John Lammy through the head.
>
> At this time the shotgun dual (sic) were within forty or fifty yards of the man who killed Sheriff Lammy with their double-barrel shotguns loaded for the occasion. Persons in the Bay area could hear the shooting of the gun battle. One man said he counted twenty-one shots fired. I made this statement against Pike County Sheriff E.W. Blades' criticism of the attempted capture of the Maxwell brothers. Any man with a thimble-full of brains knows that no one could have planned anything – meeting the outlaws by chance the way we did. The two men with the shotguns which were never fired could have changed the outcome.
>
> Signed Respectfully
> John H. Churchman

An interesting point is brought to light by Sheriff Blades. In his comments to the reporter from the *Republican*, he says that Alonzo, before shooting McNabb, had called to the deputy to surrender saying he didn't want to hurt him. McNabb replied that he would shoot till one of them fell, and fired back two shots. It was then that the younger Maxwell shot him. Blades also speculated that shooting Churchman in the leg may have been an attempt to only disable him rather than kill him. Blades was mistaken however, when he said Churchman had been shot in both legs. Only one leg was wounded.

Following the gun battle, the Maxwells resorted to an old trick. They stole two of the three horses belonging to Sheriff Lammy and Deputy Churchman and made their escape. To ensure they wouldn't be followed by someone on McNabb's horse, they shot it.

As the Maxwells rode toward the river, they were watched by Mike Fisher, one of Blades' posse members from Pike County. He had heard the firing and came galloping towards the sound of the fight. Because they were mounted, he logically assumed that these two he saw were posse members because he knew that the Maxwells were described as being afoot. He had no way of knowing at that distance who they were, but got a pretty good hint when they fired at him. He returned their fire, but they kept riding on as though the field was burning behind them. Two others of Blades' posse also saw the riders, but because they recognized the horses as belonging to Lammy and Churchman, they did not take up the chase or shoot at them.

Of the events that followed, accounts differ. One story says that riding like fury, they rode to Mozier Landing where they used a stolen skiff to cross the Mississippi to the Missouri side. Another story says that they rode to Hamburg Bay (the opposite direction from Mozier) and forced the operator of a whiskey boat, at gunpoint, to convey them across the river. When they landed in Missouri, they returned the revolver and rifle they had taken from him, but kept theirs pointed at him until he was well out into the river again.

Regardless which story was the more accurate, the Maxwells were once again sought for murdering a law officer and were loose in the countryside where the advantages belonged to them. There was no doubt in the minds of those that knew these fugitives that the Maxwells would once again fight to the death before being taken prisoners.

JOHN LAMMY'S FUNERAL

THE SHOOT-OUT THAT RESULTED in the death of John Lammy became known as "The Battle of Fox Creek". By any name the result was the same; John Lammy, a popular person and respected lawman, was dead.

Lammy in his early years had been a school teacher in Calhoun County employed at three different schools. His level of articulation and excellent composition ability were evident in his writings (see the Foreword of this book). His penmanship was meticulous also. Well-fitted for a writing career, when the opportunity presented itself, he left teaching to become the first editor of the *Calhoun Herald*, the newspaper in Hardin. At the time of his death he was in his seventh year as Sheriff of Calhoun County. To be sure he was never far from his work if he were needed, Lammy lived in the rooms above the Calhoun County Jail in Hardin.

The stone jailhouse still stands today in very good condition and continues to serve as the jail. Lammy lived on the second floor.
Photo: Les Kruger

John was never married, but it was no secret that many of the town's single ladies would fix for him fruit baskets or gifts of baked goods in an effort to catch his attention. Besides other relatives, his closest survivors were his 78 year old father, Solomon Lammy, his two brothers, William and Chittic, and his two sisters, Mary and Sarah. It was an interesting coincidence that his sisters had the same names as those of Milton and Charles Coleman.

The community was shaken and saddened when it received the news. John had been a popular and prominent person in the town and area. He was perceived as a very fair man and he went out of his way to make folks' lives better. At Christmas he was the one to put up a community Christmas tree and to provide gifts for children he knew would not otherwise have had any. In his role of sheriff, he was, by the virtue of the job description, also the tax-collector for property taxes. Rather than have to evict a delinquent for being un-able to pay, John often paid the taxes from his own pocket and had the person sign a note of indebtedness to himself. His 1881 account book revealed such debts in the four digits. It took more than four years after his death for his trustees to close all these accounts. Most of the long delay was trying to collect on behalf of his estate from those who privately owed John money.

The community he served so diligently and with such integrity did not forget him. He was buried the day after he was shot. His funeral was widely attended by friends and family along with the people of Hardin and the close outlying farming community. Officials of the county were present as were dignitaries from several surrounding counties. His remains were carried to Hardin Cemetery where he was interred at Calhoun County's expense on a prominent knoll.

Courtesy Calhoun County Historical Society

This is the only known photo of Sheriff John Lammy.

Shortly after his burial a "Lammy Monument Association" was formed with the sole purpose of raising enough money to pay for a memorial that would reflect to generations to come how much this man was revered by Hardin's grateful citizens. It wasn't going to be difficult to accumulate a suitable amount as one resident wrote to the *Herald*: "If I am not mistaken in regard to his hold on the affection of Calhoun's people, a monument costing not less than one thousand dollars could be erected with the proceeds of a fifty cent subscription." The writer was evidently correct in his estimation. Months later they had met their goal. A tall stone was erected above his grave, one of the tallest even yet today in that cemetery. Its inscription reads:

ERECTED
TO THE MEMORY
OF
JOHN LAMMY
KILLED
While In The Discharge Of
His Duty as Sheriff of
Calhoun County.
Sept. 25, 1881.
Aged
41 Years.
Photo: Les Kruger

A tribute to Lammy was printed in the *Griggsville Independent Press* in October of the year he died. It spoke of the man as many people remembered him:

He possessed a genial disposition and an unswerving fidelity to duty ... While many times honored by his fellow citizens, he was always an honor to them; while his many friends are filled with sorrow at his untimely death, they remember with pride, his honest, upright character, his modest worth.

The words expressed in that accolade to John Lammy would never have been written about his killers.

John Lammy died intestate. The court directed that his closest relatives, including his father would be regarded as beneficiaries.

The town of Hardin, Illinois' tribute to the sheriff they respected is one of the tallest monuments that stands even today in its cemetery.
Photo: Les Kruger

CONTINUED PURSUIT of the MAXWELLS

WHEN THE SHOOTING WAS finished, the Maxwells rode off on Lammy's and Churchman's horses, but not before killing McNabb's horse to put it out of commission in an effort to slow the posse. But the posse at that point was less interested in chasing the Maxwells than it was, as Sheriff Blades put it, "to care for the dead and wounded".

That comment exacted a tirade from the local papers and, in particular from John Churchman. According to a report of the events immediately following the incident, McNabb and Churchman "…had hobbled to Roth's house, and the women were doing all that could be done for them." Nobody from Blades' posse had come to their aid. Mrs. Heavner and Rosa Roth went back down to Fox Creek to remain with the body of Sheriff Lammy until someone was able to fetch him back. A snide comment in the paper suggested that Blades' men were "actually afraid to go back to the battleground for some time."

Fox Creek doesn't always have water in it, especially in the fall. Lammy's niece, Molly (Lammy) Weaver, later commented that the sheriff was killed under a buckeye tree. That might have been true, but the addition that "Fox Creek ran red to the river" is no doubt an exaggeration since it is highly improbable that there was even any water flowing that time of year. Photo: Les Kruger

The *Daily Illinois State Register* out of Springfield reported on October 4, 1881 that following Sheriff Lammy's death, Sheriff Blades of Pike County went to Springfield for an audience with Illinois Governor Cullom. As a result, the governor ordered an additional $500 reward for the capture of the Maxwells and "ordered that such arms and ammunition be placed at the disposal of Mr. Blades as he may need to properly arm a posse."

It was assumed that the outlaws would use a skiff and take the fastest route away from trouble – downriver. With that idea in mind, Chief Kennett of St. Louis along with six detectives left on the tug *Susie Hazard* to travel upstream. The idea was to meet the Maxwells as they floated downstream in a skiff. Kennett and his posse were described as "armed to the teeth and determined to take the murderers dead or alive".

At Alton, Illinois, Kennett was informed that instead of going downstream as suspected, the Maxwells had worked their way upstream and had last been seen eight or ten miles below Cap-au-Gris, about thirty miles above Alton. There they had abandoned their skiff and taken to the woods in Lincoln County in Missouri. Chief Kennett now switched boats as the water above Alton was too low for the *Suzie Hazard*. He and his troop boarded a smaller vessel called *Truant* about 11 o'clock the morning of September 28th.

The murderers were reported to have a twenty-four hour head start from the point where they left the river. In a burst of optimism, the Quincy *Daily Whig* suggested that this was nothing because the area was "alive with armed men". The *Whig's* hopefulness was shared by Chief Kennett who claimed that he expected that within a day or two the Maxwells would be captured. Sheriff Blades by this point had also joined Kennett. He too agreed with the probability of an early arrest.

The *Dora*, a Mississippi steamboat was pressed into service to scour the shoreline looking for them also, but it was expected that they were well hidden in the woods. There were no further sightings on either the Mississippi or the Illinois Rivers.

Besides the show of force on the Mississippi River, other lawmen were converging on the area and were in communication with the Lincoln County sheriff. The Illinois sheriffs of Jersey County and St. Clair County each traveled to Calhoun with a posse. The total reward money of $2,200 had definite results increasing the size of the posses. Unsure of whether the Maxwells were still in Missouri or if they had re-crossed back to Illinois, as many places as possible were posted with guards.

The Maxwells, it seemed, weren't being nearly as cautious after this last round of shooting as they had been after the Coleman killings. According to the Quincy *Daily Whig* of October 5, 1881, they were quite visible even though the law had not yet caught up to them. They had been in a small village (which that paper failed to name) and in the saloon ordered a round of drinks for the crowd in the bar. The "loafers" in the tavern (as the *Whig* refers to the saloon patrons) drank the round, but the Maxwells didn't. (Both Ed and Lon had been described by their Joliet Prison records as "temperate", neither drinking nor smoking.)

There's some confusion about which type of rifles the Maxwells were carrying. The *Whig* stated they were armed with a Henry rifle. Before the gunfight, deputy Roberts said he held their Winchester. In a researched article a hundred years later, Sheriff Lammy's great nephew, Chittick Lammy, found reference to them having a Sharps 45.70 caliber rifle which was a buffalo gun. The *Whig* went on to say they also had a "field glass", using it to detect their pursuers from a distance. ("Field glass" was a term used for our equivalent of a bin-ocular, although it may have only held one eye-piece on a telescoping tube). There may have been some merit to this claim as the same item had been indicated earlier by other sources back in Wisconsin.

The NEBRASKA CAPTURE

NOBODY WAS MORE ANXIOUS to see the Maxwell boys in manacles once again than was Sheriff J.O. Anderson of Henderson County. For him, the hunt didn't end when they left his jurisdiction following the burglaries and horse thefts. When he learned about the killing of the Coleman brothers in Wisconsin, he was immediately on his way up there to lend his knowledge about the bandits' habits. He was anxious to assist the Pepin County efforts in Wisconsin any way he could.

Before the Durand murders, he had sent out through the postal service to other sheriff departments, post cards depicting the Maxwells' likenesses with the express warnings that these men were heavily armed and dangerous. He emphasized that they were desperate men willing to stop at nothing.

The cards Anderson had mailed were received by Milt Coleman and Miletus Knight in Wisconsin. They also reached E.W. Blades and John Lammy in Illinois. And they reached Sheriff Joseph Kilian of Hall County, Nebraska.

Joseph Kilian was a music-loving member of the Czech community of Grand Island. (In fact, the 1880 census for Hall County records him as a Prussian.) On Monday night, the 7th of November, he was playing with his orchestra for a dance in Liederkranz Hall when a fellow constable from a neighbouring precinct brought him some compelling information.

Two men had requested lodging at the farmhouse of William Needfeldt claiming to be goose hunters out from Hastings, a town about twenty-five miles to the south. For several reasons they aroused the suspicions of the farmer. For starters, the heavy weapons these men were carrying were not appropriate for hunting geese. They were rifles rather than shotguns. Recalling information he had seen in a fairly recent Milwaukee newspaper, Needfeldt checked the discarded edition. After comparing the description it gave of the Maxwells with the two men he had met, and deciding it was a match, he sent word to Kilian about his discovery.

The reward on the Maxwells' heads was by now quite heavy. Kilian knew of the fate of the Coleman brothers and John Lammy. He was going to take no chances no matter how much money was at stake. Before setting out he recruited Chris Staal, another law officer from Merrick County, August Nitsch, a young man who made cigars for a living in Grand Island, and a neighbour of Mr. Needfeldt, Ludwig Shultz. Arming themselves with several revolvers and double-barreled shotguns, they arrived at Needfeldt's place about 5 am.

The farmhouse was small with only two rooms. Ed and Alonzo occupied one. Passing themselves off as goose hunters also, Kilian and his small posse feigned the need for some coffee to refresh themselves before the geese were over the fields. Ed and Alonzo had still been sleeping on the floor, their Winchesters close beside them and each had a revolver under his pillow. On the entrance of the lawmen, they became instantly vigilant.

Kilian and his men tried to put the Maxwells off their guard with some general small-talk about hunting and the weather. When he asked them questions about Hastings, he knew he was not getting the right answers. This was the clincher that the boys were not who they said they were. While they were getting dressed, Kilian noticed that the younger one put his stockings on while his feet were still under the bedding. Knowing that Lon Maxwell was missing a toe on his right foot, the sheriff was sure the man was trying to hide his one identifiable physical anomaly. After they finished dressing, Ed stood by the corner of the room with his right hand comfortably clutching his Winchester. Lon, either feeling the need for a nature call or just wanting to check their horses in the stable, left his rifle, hat and coat and walked casually out to the barn. Evidently, he was not alarmed by the presence of the interlopers.

Kilian instantly recognized that this was the opportunity he needed. With Lon outside, he and his men would be able to contend better with them one at a time. He approached Ed, who was by now completely off his guard having determined that these four men really were fellow goose hunters.

"I want to talk with you", he said moving toward the unwary Maxwell. His change of demeanor instantly alerted Ed that something was amiss. He quickly brought up his rifle as though to shoot, but Kilian grabbed Ed around the body binding his arms, and slammed him to the floor.

Despite his smallish stature, Ed was wiry, surprisingly muscular and very quick. As the two fought on the floor, Ed tried desperately to escape Kilian's hold. Kicking and thrashing, he made every attempt to free himself, all the while throwing the odd wild punch.

This was an arrest and was not intended to be a sporting event. Ed Maxwell was a dangerous fellow on a good day, but cornered and pinioned this way, he was a menacing, desperate man. Immediately Nitsch and Needfeldt jumped into the skirmish and made sure Ed's rifle was safely wrestled from his grasp. Maxwell was eventually subdued and the three deputies held him under control. Kilian hid both rifles in the other room and assumed that these were all the arms the Maxwells had with them. When he returned to the room where Ed was guarded, he found his men now had Ed on his back on the floor. While Kilian was in the other room, Ed had worked himself along the bed where he had got hold of both his revolvers. Before he had a chance to use them, the deputies pounced on him once more. Taking no more chances, Kilian handcuffed the felon.

A week later, after having time to reflect, Kilian told reporters

Ed was one of the most muscular men for his size he had encountered, and that it was all they could do to handle him.

But for Ed, being down didn't mean being out. Assessing the seriousness of his situation, he let out a number of Indian war whoops in an effort to warn his brother. Kilian was afraid that this would alert Lon and give him enough time to escape. Wanting to effectively capture both of them, the sheriff stepped cautiously out the farmhouse door to look for the younger outlaw. Nitsch remained in the doorway with his shotgun at the ready.

Courtesy Pepin County Historical Society

Wiry and quick, Ed was not going to be an easy capture. By late 1881 he was as wild as this photo portrays. Every lawman was warned that he was dangerous and heavily armed. They were not to risk taking him alone.

Lon wasn't planning an escape. He was racing to his brother's defense with his revolver in his hand. In the half-light of daybreak, Kilian saw Lon sprinting across the yard towards the door of the farmhouse. Kilian ordered him to halt, but in response the young bandit fired a hastily aimed shot at the lawman. But Kilian had anticipated such an action and jumped back into Needfeldt's kitchen in time to dodge the bullet. Fortunately he was wearing a shirt that fit loosely on his body because the bullet passed through his clothing between his chest and his shirt. He immediately closed the door partially behind him and stepped to one side with his foot against it. Lon reached the door and gave it a kick, no doubt expecting it to open up so he could let fly some lead. But it only opened about three inches and when he looked in he found himself instead looking down the barrels of Nitsch's shotgun. Beating a hurried retreat, he ran around the corner of the house and went to a window.

Nitsch had anticipated this move and just as Lon raised his pistol to shoot, Nitsch aimed at Lon's head and pulled the trigger. Both cartridges in the shotgun failed to fire. Lon got off a hurried, ineffectual shot that lodged in a leg of the kitchen table. However, he sensed that he was outnumbered and outgunned. He was the one that was vulnerable out in the open. The posse had the protection of the inside of the house. Seeing his disadvantage, Alonzo turned and fled.

The sheriff and his men remained inside not daring to show themselves at the door or windows for fear of being shot at by Lon. Moments later another face appeared outside the window looking in. Luckily its owner didn't linger too long or he might have been mistaken for Alonzo and been shot by the lawmen. It was Needfeldt's hired hand who had been in the barn. When he heard the shooting and commotion, he came out to investigate in time to see Lon hightailing towards the tall grass and woods as fast as he could.

Now that it was certain that Alonzo had made an escape, Kilian turned his attention to his handcuffed prize still lying on the kitchen floor of the farmhouse. Ed was unceremoniously loaded onto a lumber wagon and hauled back to Grand Island. Along the route Nitsch kept his shotgun cocked half-expecting to be ambushed from the tall grass by Lon. This served to anger Ed who challenged the young deputy to a fight. However, the lawmen were not going to be distracted by any of his antics. By 7:30 that morning Ed Maxwell was once again safely behind bars in the Grand Island jail cells.

After being frisked, Ed was found to be carrying about thirty cartridges for his Winchester sewn up in an outside pocket of the jacket he wore. As well in his possession, he had a silver watch, two horse blankets, and about two dollars in cash. The two blankets were the last bit of thievery the boys had done. He was inaccurately described in the local newspaper as being five feet eight inches tall. In fact, he was about five inches shorter than that. He was said to have a moustache and chin whiskers, so it wasn't true that he had tried to disguise himself by shaving as had been suggested earlier by another newspaper.

Kilian seized two 1876 model Winchester rifles and two revolvers at the farmhouse. Bullet moulds for the guns and a machine for manufacturing the cartridges were found too. The machine was complete in every detail having a cap extractor and a re-capper, a ladle in which to melt the lead, and a crimper for molding the brass around the ball.

At the jail Ed demanded of Kilian, "Why did you arrest me?" Kilian told him then that he was under arrest for horse stealing. For the time being, that was the only charge Ed thought he was going to be facing.

A search was mounted for Alonzo after Ed was locked behind bars. Several teams of posse members scoured the Platt Valley, but the hunt proved to be fruitless. He had taken no chances of being jailed alongside his older brother. No doubt he had once again headed for the more heavily forested area to wait for dark before moving on. He was known to be an excellent marksman particularly with a rifle, but it was also known of him that, without Ed beside him for encouragement and support, he was a complete coward, incapable of being decisive. Kilian knew that when Lon escaped he had a belt containing about 100 cartridges, but they were for the rifle he left behind, not his revolver. Ironically, Ed had nearly all the shells for the revolvers with him.

Joseph Kilian wasted no time alerting the Wisconsin authorities that he had captured Ed Maxwell. After all, the large reward would go a long way to making a notable difference in his bank account. Miletus Knight wired back that he would leave on the first available train. Kilian felt it was a good time to let his prisoner know he was going to face a murder charge. Ed reacted by vehemently insisting he was not Ed Maxwell or Williams. He was a victim of mistaken identity. When he was informed that Durand had been telegraphed with news of his imprisonment, he replied, "You can be damned for all the good that will do. I don't care. Besides, I'm not the first man who has been taken for a Williams boy." (On this point Ed was accurate. Several others had been detained on suspicion of being a Maxwell because of some physical similarities). Ed said there were a lot of people in the world who resembled the Williams and that they hadn't got them all yet. (Ed was still using the alias of "Williams" rather than Maxwell.)

While he was being detained at Grand Island awaiting the arrival of Sheriff Knight from Durand, Ed granted an interview to the reporter from *The Globe-Democrat* among others. It seemed there was a line-up of journalists wanting to gain access to Ed. Those who were to be accommodated had a chalk mark placed on their hat by the sheriff to acknowledge being granted an audience with the murderer.

Usually not one to be shy, Ed this time was somewhat uncommunicative and reticent about revealing too much. Asked to comment on the rumours surrounding the doings of himself and Lon, Ed replied, "A still tongue makes a wise head." He claimed that he and his "partner" were there only on a hunting expedition.

When asked why he and the other man carried the type of weapons they did, he answered that they wanted to be ready for whatever type of game came their way.

"Were you from Hastings?"
"That's what we told those who questioned us."
"Did you come west over the U.P. on Monday?"
"Yes, sir."
"At what place did you leave the train – near a station?"
"The railroad men can probably tell what the name of it is."

Throughout the interview, Maxwell was considerably less than truthful. Some of the reporter's questions were leading, but Ed refused to be taken in by most. On the question of the train station, it was already known that they had come west on a freight train the previous Monday and that as they approached Lockwood Station about five miles east of Grand Island, they had jumped from the moving train. Since their father and the rest of their family were now living approximately fifty-five miles away in Osco in Kearney County, it was assumed that the boys were on their way to visit them.

"At what point on the Missouri River did you cross?"

"At Omaha."

"Have you any relations or friends in the state?"

"Only acquaintances ."

"In what part of the state do those acquaintances live?"

"I prefer not to answer."

"Was your partner a relative, or merely a friend?"

"An acquaintance."

"Where was the acquaintance formed?"

"In the east – Ohio."

"You were accused of horse stealing; was it true?"

"We had no horses with us, nor any in Nebraska that I had ever taken."

"If you were innocent, why had you so desperately resisted arrest?"

"Well, a man might be fearing arrest for a crime of minor importance, and possibly for crimes he was not guilty of."

"Would you object to stating what crime you had committed and where?"

"I decline to answer."

"Would it not be better to suffer the extent of the law for a slight crime than to deliberately shoot a man down who might be attempting his arrest?"

"Well, it's a bad thing to shoot a man, and I wouldn't like to do it unless I thought I had call, but after a man had been in prison and gotten out everybody gave him the cold shoulder and that was not pleasant."

"Was that your experience? Have you ever been in prison?"

"I prefer not to answer."

"What arms has your partner with him now?"

"Two large Navy revolvers and he is the best shot with a rifle or revolver that I ever saw. In shooting at a mark I have seen him do things that I thought impossible for any man to do."

"Did you yourself resist arrest?"

"I had done all I could to prevent it, and if I had more room and had not been taken by surprise, somebody would have gotten hurt. I would never have been taken if I had had the least intimation of the object of my captors and had been out of doors. I would have defied them all."

"If you are an innocent man, why do you object to giving your name and where you are from?"

"I don't want it to get into the newspapers, out of consideration for the feelings of my friends back east."

"It is said that your partner had shot at the sheriff and missed him."

"Possibly, but it was dark and he was excited or the sheriff would never have escaped."

Not a great deal of information was gleaned about Ed through the conversation. However, he did leave an indelible impression on the reporter who found him to be quiet, mild-mannered and even obedient in jail. It was thought that the last trait might be the result of being institutionalized in Joliet prison for six years previously. He revealed himself to be articulate and easy to talk with. Something that was often noted about any conversation with Ed was that he was "cool and gentlemanly, using the best of language, -- no oaths, no slang, no boasting". Ed was almost never heard to swear or use coarse, vulgar language. He was found to be "gentlemanly in his demeanor and a man who would create a favorable impression among strangers." This last part might have been true as long as he wasn't carrying revolvers or rifles.

In many ways Ed had his own sense of honour. One reporter asked him if, on a particular point, he was lying. "I don't lie, Sir," he replied. "I guess I haven't a great while in this world, and I don't want to add lying to my other sins."

Strangely, as the reporter was preparing to leave, Ed asked him if he had any religious articles to read.

The correspondent who visited Ed in the Grand Island jail left with the impression that Maxwell did not believe he would ever be taken back to Wisconsin. He seemed to possess self-confidence perhaps inspired, as the reporter suggested, that Ed felt there might be some "outside assistance" forthcoming.

Never one to quit in the face of the authorities though, it was discovered that during his first night in his cell, he tampered with the lock mechanism. He actually managed to partially turn one of the tumblers. In the morning Sheriff Kilian asked him what he had been doing. "Nothing," he replied, "the lock is worthless in the first place and likely to become broken."

The search went on for Alonzo throughout the adjacent counties. The only traces that were found at all were two sightings near Aurora in Hamilton County. The first was by a farmer. At the time Lon was wearing a duck-hunting vest that he had no doubt stolen along his journey to stay warm. According to the farmer, no arms were visible, but he did keep his right hand inside the front of his coat. This was considered by those that knew him to mean his revolver was readily available should he feel threatened. The second sighting was by a young boy. Maxwell gave the boy money and sent him into a store to buy him some food. Since then, nothing more of him surfaced.

It was to be a long time before anything more was heard of Alonzo Maxwell.

MISTAKEN IDENTITIES

IT WAS EASY FOR Ed to tell the authorities in Nebraska that they were mistaken about who he was. It wasn't the only occasion that someone else was taken to be a Maxwell or a Williams. After all, a working man's clothing or an outfit worn by farmers or hunters looked pretty much the same on anybody and, at a distance, who would be able to tell?

Except for their smallish stature, there was nothing terribly remarkable about the Maxwells that would stand out in a crowd. So when everyone was hunting the Eau Galle River bottoms, it's not surprising that there were several innocent fellows taken for the fugitives. The tramp in the haycock near Knapp was only one example. Another unfortunate wanderer was walking along the brush inside the fence owned by a farmer named McGilton. He just happened to be close to where they were looking for Maxwells. A Captain Baker who was posted to that area saw the man and let fire a shotgun loaded with buckshot as the fellow was climbing over the fence. It's reported by the *Courier* that the man "fell off the fence as though dead, but soon got up and 'lit out', using considerable profane and vulgar language to the guard." While it was assumed at the time that the man was a Maxwell, it was discovered later that they were not in that vicinity at all. Fortunately for the wayfarer, the inability of

Baker to make positive identification of his quarry was exceeded by his poor skill with a firearm.

One enterprising young man named Vance took advantage of the Maxwell notoriety early in their careers in 1875 and tried to turn it to his advantage. Working on an area ranch near Blandinsville, he stole money and a revolver from his co-workers. To shift blame away from himself, he threw all the ranch hands' pants into the farmyard, including his own. When the discovery was made, blame was quickly attached to the Maxwells until someone discovered the stolen revolver in Vance's boot. Since there was nothing outstanding about the gun, he almost got away with calling it his own. But the real owner had done a repair job on the piece and used an unusual spring on the mechanism. When the pistol was broken down, sure enough, the spring convicted the Maxwell impersonator.

Another instance occurred in New Ulm, Minnesota when a tramp was caught with a stolen harness. Thinking that they had captured Ed Maxwell, the authorities there held him in tight security. They knew of Ed's propensity for attempting escapes. Sheriff Peterson of Durand journeyed to New Ulm to make sure, but it definitely wasn't Ed. It was S.T. King who was described as a "tough citizen on general principles" but not of the caliber of a Maxwell. King was ordered to take Maxwell's reservation in the Iron Bar Hotel for a few weeks for his crime.

Most of the traveling to identify potential Maxwell captures was done by Miletus Knight. In fact he was away so much that financially it was becoming a drain both on the county and on Knight. Much of it was out-of-pocket expenses for the lawman, but Pepin County kicked in funds as well to offset the travel bills.

There was one very interesting case that caught the media attention for some time due to its unique flavour. In Milwaukee a man who called himself William Kuhl was arrested by Deputy-Sheriff Max Greding on suspicion of being Lon Maxwell. The local newspaper, The Milwaukee *Wisconsin*, indicated that the man was indeed Alonzo.

Other people arrived from the northern part of the state who knew Maxwell also and they agreed that the man in custody was Lon. To add more positive identification, the hat Alonzo had dropped the night of the Coleman murders was shown to the man. It was still decorated with the mourning crepe. At the sight of the hat, it was said the man reddened and choked with emotion. He was asked to try on the hat. He did with a perfect fit. By this time the Milwaukee authorities were convinced they had the right Maxwell in custody.

This is a later photo of Alonzo Maxwell. Even people who knew him fairly well confused William Kuhl with Maxwell since their features were so similar.

Their assurance was cemented when Henry Coleman arrived at the Milwaukee jail. Henry, brother of the murdered Milt and Charles, had worked with Lon in Knapp and is said to have known him fairly well. The two had even practiced target shooting together on at least one occasion. When he saw the man in jail, Henry greeted him with, "Hello, old fellow, you are the man we are looking for and if you ain't Lon, then you have his skin drawn over you. Don't you remember when we used to practice shooting pistols out on the railroad track?" By now, all Kuhl's denials were futile.

Not everyone though believed that the man in custody was Alonzo Maxwell. There was one small problem. This man had ten toes. If he was Lon, he should have been missing one digit from his right foot. For some reason this one convincing feature was overlooked.

Miletus Knight arrived shortly afterward and with Henry, escorted the man to Menonomie where he was imprisoned.

Before Kuhl left Milwaukee, the sheriff there stated he was glad there had been a "positive" identity. His reasoning was that Kuhl should be "… thoroughly identified before he is taken to the scene of that terrible Coleman tragedy and placed in the dangerous position of being attacked by a mob …" Prophetic words!! It was almost as though the authorities might have expected a murderer such as Alonzo to be lynched if brought back to Durand.

But then, there was that missing toe!

While Kuhl was housed in the Menonomie jail, M. J. Huggins of Arkansaw was brought in to help identify the prisoner. Huggins had lived at Hersey and knew both Williams brothers well. While Dr. Baker amputated Lon's toe, Huggins was present and held Lon's hand during the surgery. He claimed that Kuhl was definitely not Alonzo.

Similarly, G. W. Reynolds, the telegraph operator at Hersey, was brought to the jail. He too instantly recognized that the man being held was not Lon Williams.

Even Lon's father-in-law, William Thompson, was brought in to identify the man. In an interesting twist, Thompson was so vehement in denying that this was Alonzo that it was at first thought he was over-doing it in an effort to protect Lon, which only served to heap more suspicion on Kuhl.

The man continued to insist he wasn't a Maxwell. He claimed to have a sister and that he had been working in the area close to where he'd been discovered. Such insistence could not be completely ignored. Miletus Knight, an inveterate professional, would leave no stone unturned even if it meant searching for a man's innocence if not his guilt. Kuhl's sister was summonsed from Milwaukee. Knight also requested the man for whom Kuhl said he had recently worked. The employer couldn't make the journey, but instead his son, a man named Miller, arrived to look over the suspect. Miller stated that William Kuhl had indeed worked for his father and could clearly recall that on Sunday July 10[th,] the day of the Durand massacre, Kuhl was working on their farm. Miller gave his statement in a straightforward fashion that convinced Knight the farmer was being truthful.

Following that, Kuhl was brought to an adjoining room where he was permitted to meet his sister. Those who were present had no further doubt about the man's true identity. After being freed to leave, Kuhl and his supporters indicated they were pleased with the treatment afforded them at Menonomie as opposed to what they had been subjected in Milwaukee.

Kuhl's tale didn't end with his release. By mid-November the Milwaukee *Sentinel* reported that after being detained there for weeks, Kuhl was launching a law suit against the county and its officers for false imprisonment. It was anticipated that he would sue for something between $50,000 and $100,000. The case was in litigation for eight years and was finally settled in Kuhl's favour. He was awarded more than $5300.

It was generally agreed that William Kuhl did bear an uncanny likeness to Alonzo Maxwell. One newspaper, *The State Journal* reacted with an editorial:

> Kuhl's resemblance to Williams is unfortunate, but it would appear that it is only a resemblance. At all events, the Milwaukee police should have been less hasty, for there was real danger of a lynching bee in Pepin County, and it was simply murderous to subject their prisoner to it...

In defense of its citizens, the Pepin *Courier* shot back, "The disposition of our people and the Menonomie people is to give the murderers a fair trial, and no person arrested will be molested, especially if the question of identity is at all in doubt."

Clearly the good people of Durand had no doubt about Ed's identity the afternoon that they took him out and hanged him.

The DURAND LYNCHING

···

WHETHER OR NOT ED thought he'd see Wisconsin again, he did. Sheriff Miletus Knight and Deputy Sheriff Henry Coleman, the younger of the surviving Coleman brothers, journeyed to Nebraska to make positive identification and to take back the prisoner. With them on the trip back was Sheriff Joseph Kilian who no doubt wanted to collect his reward money as well as seeing the finale in Ed's saga.

On arriving at Grand Island, Henry was introduced to Maxwell on the pretense of him being a young lawyer newly arrived from Omaha to offer assistance. Because he knew Ed wouldn't recognize him, he wanted to try to pump him for information that they might otherwise not be able to get under different circumstances. After an hour-long conversation in Ed's cell, he learned almost nothing they didn't already know. Ed persisted in calling it a case of mistaken identity, that he was being erroneously held as one of the infamous "Williams" brothers.

There wasn't going to be another blunder of identification as had happened in the case of Kuhl. To ensure accuracy, Knight and Kilian had Ed's photograph taken to be sent for a positive ID at Joliet prison.

Courtesy Pepin County Historical Society

For this photo Ed worked hard to make himself appear unrecogniz-able. Compare this picture with the one in the chapter of "The Nebraska Capture" which was evidently taken afterwards. He's wearing the same clothing.

At the photographer's studio Ed was less than cooperative. The first time he lowered his shoulders and screwed up his face in a de-liberate attempt to distort his features making himself less recogniz-able. After Knight threatened that they would have his photo 'dead or alive', he allowed a picture. But his hair was long and unkempt and he had not shaved recently, so he photographed with a rather scruffy appearance. After a haircut and shave his third photograph gave a much truer impression.

The photo was immediately sent to Joliet for identification. While waiting for a response, they moved Maxwell to Omaha and housed him in the jail there, a larger, more secure facility. Just before leaving Grand Island, Sheriff Knight received a telegram from Hastings, Nebraska. It was from Ed's father, David Maxwell in Osco. The elder

Maxwell requested that they hold Ed in Grand Island at least until the following day to allow him an opportunity to visit his son. The telegram was shown to Ed, but the prisoner denied that this was his father. Evidently he was sticking to his story of "mistaken identity". Eventually Ed decided to relinquish the charade. In Omaha he asked Knight to telegraph his father asking the elder Maxwell to meet him in Omaha, that he would like to see his father. The meeting did not happen. Early the next morning he was on his way to Wisconsin with no time for a brief reunion.

Because at first he denied David Maxwell was his father, Ed never again had an opportunity to see him before he died. His father's tombstone lies on the ground in Osco Cemetery. David died in 1887 at age 55. The small wording at the bottom reads:
He took thee from a world of care
In everlasting bliss to share.
Photo: Les Kruger

By the time they arrived a dispatch from Joliet was waiting. According to the Joliet record clerk, S.R. Wettmore, the photo definitely was Ed Maxwell, although he thought it to be a poor picture.

The entourage arrived in Menonomie at 4 pm on Thursday, November 17 on the C.St.P, M.&O. train. They had been expected earlier, so there was some concern when they were not there to board the 3 pm stage for Durand. But when their train finally pulled in to the Menonomie station, a large crowd had already gathered to get a look at the killer. Despite having this dangerous murderer in their midst, the throng was quiet and orderly.

Maxwell was removed from the train and taken straight to the local jail. All the while he was closely guarded and it was reported that he was "heavily ironed". Usually an attention seeker, this time Ed seemed somewhat cowed and frightened by the presence of the crowd. He seemed to expect trouble despite the silence of those assembled. He may have sensed that beneath the restrained composure of the onlookers, this bunch harboured a lot of hostility towards him. Yet he maintained an outward air of calmness.

Sheriff Severson did the honours of locking him in jail. Nobody was allowed into his cell that night, but by Friday morning several reporters were once again permitted to interview him. As on all past occasions, the ones who were granted an up-close audience with Ed were struck first by his rather diminutive frame. It was always assumed that anyone who could cause that much mayhem must surely be a huge person, a man of monstrous proportions. But at five feet, three inches, they were always taken aback at just how small Ed Maxwell really was. Again in Menonomie, as in Grand Island, he was described as "gentlemanly in address, easy and self-possessed in conversation ... with nothing to indicate the bold and desperate character of the man."

Clean shaven, except for the moustache and imperial chin whiskers, his only other outward feature worth noting was his new brown felt hat that added to his cocksure demeanor. He was now 28 years old.

Back in his old stomping grounds where he knew he would be

easily recognized, he no longer maintained the charade of mistaken identity. He acknowledged he was Ed Williams, alias Maxwell, an obvious interesting reversal he must have enjoyed. He spoke freely about the flight he and Lon had made through the Eau Galle River bottoms following the Coleman shootings. He acknowledged one other piece of information that until then had only been intimated. He said that the night they shot the Colemans, they had come to Durand to "get even" with Sheriff Miletus Knight. It had been Knight who had removed the horse they had left at Mrs. Senz' place in Eau Galle. And, of course, they knew it was Miletus Knight who had interrogated Fannnie prior to her going into the painful labour of childbirth that ultimately led to her death. Alonzo was on a trail of vengeance that day. Their contempt for Knight was emphasized as Ed referred to the lawman as "Grandmother Knight".

As would be expected, his version of the events the night of the killings was slightly different. He claimed they felt they were being surrounded in Durand after being discovered there, that they met the Colemans not knowing who they were, and that the Colemans fired on them first. According to Ed, he and Alonzo fired in self-defense. As for the Illinois killing, he denied having anything to do with the death of Sheriff Lammy. He claimed they were not in that area at all. He did not account for the fact that someone there had spoken with them and recognized them. Realistically, had Ed been planning to plead "self-defense" for the Coleman killings, how would he have been able to weasel out of the Lammy murder? His only hope would have been to maintain he was never there. Accordingly, he stuck to that story until the bitter end.

One other interesting interview was granted before Maxwell left Menonomie. The mother of the two dead Coleman brothers was allowed to confront her sons' killer in his cell. Probably this was granted by special dispensation as a result of Henry's role in the search and in escorting Maxwell back from Nebraska. Alice Coleman looked the murderer in the eyes and asked, "How could you kill my boys?"

Ed replied in an apologetic tone, "I am truly sorry I did so. I did not know them at all. We were not after them." He went on to explain to her, "Our idea was to get to Sheriff Knight's house that night, catch him in his bed, get the drop on him and make him take us to where the horse he captured from us was concealed. He would have gone, I am sure, but if he hadn't, he'd have had to die." Considering Alice Coleman's straightforward manner, this was no doubt a very unsatisfactory response to her tortured question, but it was all she would ever get from Ed by way of an explanation.

On Saturday, November 19th in Menonomie *The News*, reported that Ed was taken late the previous day (the 18th) to Durand to appear in court. Although there had been a throng of curious onlookers at the Menonomie jail to see Maxwell that morning, the paper noted "there was no excitement whatever, and the disposition of the public is to let the law take its course." The ironic understatement of that comment would not soon be forgotten.

The historic Durand Courthouse looks virtually the same today as that fateful afternoon in November 1881. Photo: Les Kruger

Only the week before, the La Crosse *Republican Leader* had printed an article stating "the Pepin County authorities are 'biling' over with anxiety to be revenged on somebody for the brutal murder of the Coleman brothers ..." The Pepin *Courier* responded saying it wasn't true. "They propose to give every man a fair trial, and if guilty, make him suffer – if not, no harm will come to him."

On Friday the 18th of November Ed Maxwell was returned to the town where he had helped kill the Colemans. A large crowd had gathered at the river where the stage on the other side of the river would be steam-ferried across the Chippewa. They wanted to see just what this infamous murderer looked like who had so disrupted their tranquil town on a quiet summer night. After the stage was transported across the river, Maxwell was led through the group by the lawmen and was taken to the Durand jail where he was watched carefully under a heavy guard.

Once again Ed granted an interview to the local newspaper and, as usual the reporter's first impression was about the small stature of the man. "Ed is not so large a man as has been supposed. His height 5 feet and one inch and weight about 140 lbs, body solid and compact, and he possessed great muscular power." It was difficult to believe that despite his reputation, Ed did not appear in the least to be a fierce person.

Ed was originally scheduled to appear in court the following morning, November 19th at ten o'clock. Instead he was re-scheduled for 2 pm in the afternoon. Although the reasons why the time was changed have never been made clear, this alteration of the schedule has had a profound effect on the reporting of what happened that day in Durand, both in 1881, and ever since to the present day. No other single detail has led to more mis-information and exaggeration than the results of that four-hour delay. The reasons for that will be made clear in the next chapter.

Ed's appearance in the court-room was attended and reported by the journalist from The Pepin *Courier*. The room on the second floor of the courthouse was crowded with men, women and even children all pressing to get a glimpse of the notorious killer. Maxwell was brought in to appear before Justice W.B. Dyer. He was heavily ironed wearing both handcuffs and a ball-and-chain attached to one leg. He carried the ball in his hands in front of him.

Standing before the judge, he gave his correct name as William E. Maxwell. The charge was read by the Justice to which Maxwell pleaded "Not Guilty." He waived an examination and the Justice determined to commit him for trial. According to the reporters who were present in the court-room that day, no other words were spoken by Ed Maxwell in the court. A plea of "not guilty" and the decline of the examination were the only matters that were dealt with during his short appearance. In all, he probably spoke less than a dozen words. Ed was ordered to be taken back to the Durand jail.

Maxwell was under guard by Sheriff Peterson, Under-Sheriff Knight, Deputy Henry Coleman, Sheriff Kilian, Marshall Seeley and Thomas Garvin. There was no doubt that he was being well guarded. But what transpired next left that opinion open to public debate.

Just as they reached the bottom of the stairs at the front door of the courthouse, a group of men, obviously prepared for the occasion, rushed the troop of lawmen. The Sheriff and deputies were quickly marshaled away from their prisoner and herded down the main hall on the lower level. Ed was rapidly separated from anyone who might have saved him.

"Hang the son of a bitch", yelled out one of the members of the mob. About twenty-five men took part in the scramble that lasted over the next few short minutes. Several men grappled with Maxwell while others deliberately maintained the breach between the lawmen and their charge preventing them from defending Maxwell. Someone produced a noose already prepared for the occasion and slipped it over Ed's head, the 'hangman's knot' deftly placed behind his left ear.

Although the law officers resisted, they were outnumbered by a determined crowd of vigilantes who pushed them further down the hall away from the courthouse front door. Out that same door Maxwell was dragged by his executioners. Tenacious to the end, he fought vigorously with his captors knowing what awaited him. They were equally determined to see him get his "just desserts". Yanked across the front porch of the courthouse, he was then dragged kick-ing and fighting across the lawn until he was under an oak tree on the east side of the building. The rope was thrown up over a branch.

Courthouse steps where the vigilantes grabbed Ed.
Photo: L. Kruger

"Haul away", were the only other words spoken by anyone in the crowd. A dozen men pulled the rope tight and secured it by tying it around the tree trunk. Maxwell was suspended thirty feet in the air, still wearing handcuffs, still with the ball-and-chain shackled on his left leg.

For a few brief minutes the crowd stood and looked at the man swinging in the cold November air. The afternoon was dull. The sky was slightly overcast. An inch or two of snow was already on the ground and a few flakes were in the air. Gradually the crowd dis-persed. It was said that there was no talk, not even whisperings. A sense of solemnity prevailed. People just quietly walked away leav-ing Ed Maxwell dangling over the courthouse lawn.

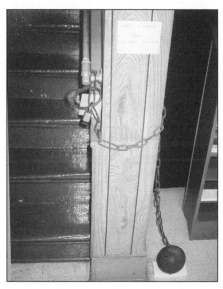

Ed's leg irons, ball and chain.

Minutes later the lawmen grouped together under the same tree staring up at the limp body. They cut him down and went through the motions of trying to detect life, but to no avail. Ed Maxwell, petty thief, burglar, horse-thief and murderer, was dead. True to the *Stillwater Messenger* prophecy, he died with his boots on.

As a legal formality, an inquiry was held over his body later that same evening. Justice A.W. Hammond instructed Under-Sheriff Miletus Knight to summons "… forthwith six good and lawful men of Pepin County …" to view the body of Ed Maxwell and "… to determine "… how, and by what means he came to his death." Knight's jurymen rendered their verdict. Hammond, who also viewed the dead Maxwell, accepted their advice. On Maxwell's inquest form he wrote "… I believed that an inquest not necessary and therefore caused the body to be burried (sic) in the Potter's field in the village cemetery in the town of Durand."

Itemized on the same inquest form are the costs for disposing of Ed. The pine box in which he was interred was $3.00 along with $2.50 to pay a man to dig the grave. It cost the county another $1.50 to haul the remains by horse-drawn wagon to the cemetery. But even with other incidentals added in, for less than ten dollars Pepin County, Wisconsin and Illinois were finally rid of Ed Maxwell.

It can never be known for sure if this is what the writer for the *Dunn County News* had in mind on July 30th of 1881 when he penned, "They are marked men and unless they flee beyond the borders of this country they will, sooner or later meet the fate they so richly deserve."

Ed's Winchester rifle when it was on loan to the Durand Courthouse Museum

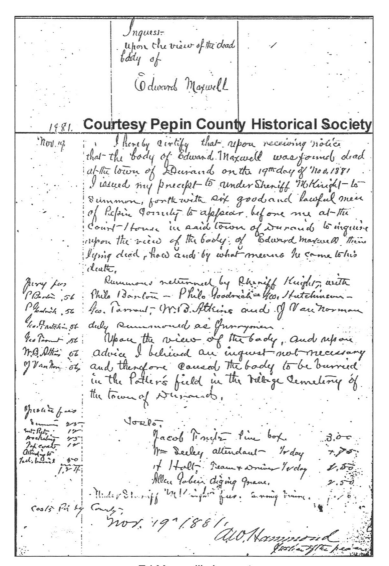

Ed Maxwell's Inquest

I hereby certify that upon receiving notice that the body of Edward Maxwell was found dead at the town of Durand on the 19th day of Nov. 1881 I issued my precept to Under Sheriff M. Knight to summon forthwith six good and lawful men of Pepin County to appear before me at the court-house in said town of Durand to inquire upon the view of the body of Edward Maxwell, there lying dead, how and by what means he came to his death.

Summons returned by Sheriff Knight with Philo Banton – Philo Goodrich – Geo. Hutchinson – Geo. Tarrant – W.B. Atkins and J. Van Norman duly summoned as jurrymen. (sic)

Upon the view of the body, and upon advice, I believed an inquest not necessary and therefore caused the body to be buried in the Potter's field in the village cemetery of the town of Durand.

Costs,

Jacob Tinitz	Pine box	3.00
Wm Seeley	attendant ¼ day	.75
H Holt	Team & Driver ½ day	1.50
Allen Jobeir (?)	diging (sic) grave	2.50

Under Sheriff M. Knight fees   (unclear)

Nov. 19, 1881

A.W. Hammond

Justice of the Peace

SENSATIONAL ST. PAUL JOURNALIST

JOURNALISTS ARE NOT MERELY writers of news stories. They are the first-line chroniclers of history. Newspapers, because of the role they serve presenting daily or weekly factual information, are often the first places researchers turn in an effort to locate truthful, accurate portrayal of events. When those reports are tainted by sloppy, irresponsible journalism, the history can become forever distorted.

Nowhere had this become more blatant than with the story of Ed Maxwell.

Ed had been originally scheduled to appear in the Durand courtroom at ten o'clock on Saturday morning, November 19th. Everyone assumed that the pre-arranged court date would go ahead as planned. Nobody anticipated things going awry as they sometimes do. To this day there is no record of what caused the time of Ed's arraignment to be postponed. But it was. And that has changed forever the historical truth the Maxwell story has received ever since.

On hearing of the capture of the notorious Ed Maxwell, the *St. Paul Pioneer Press* anticipated a "breaking news" story for its readership. The antics of the Maxwells had been fully documented over the previous years dating well back to their break-ins at the St. Croix Lumber Company in Bayport and their subsequent capture at Stillwater by Sheriff Shortall. To follow-up on the most recent story of the Nebraska capture, the *Pioneer Press* sent E.R. Johnstone, one of their top reporters, to cover the events. The *Pioneer Press* was a well known, highly respected newspaper of the day. It was a large-market paper and what it reported was often picked up by smaller newspapers and weeklies and its stories copied throughout the country. Because of its solid reputation in front-line journalism, people assumed that if it was in the *Press*, it must be true.

Johnstone, like everyone else, expected a ten o'clock appearance by Maxwell. When it didn't happen on time, he was unable apparently, to remain in Durand. He and a Mr. Carpenter left about noon for Menonomie. Perhaps the reason for their departure had something to do with the stage schedules out of Durand in order to meet the St. Paul stage or the train out of Menonomie. In any event, Johnstone left Durand fully two or three hours before Maxwell was hung.

On reaching Menonomie, Johnstone learned via telegraphed information that Ed Maxwell had been lynched by a mob. Not wishing to lose a good story, or incur the wrath of an expectant editor, Johnstone wrote his version based on the skimpy details he'd received and evidently embellished the tale with prodigious, imaginary details culled from his brief visit to Durand.

Johnstone's version was a damning portrayal of rabid Durand citizens creating a frenzied scene of mob violence. Virtually none of the facts were correct. He described the incident in the most sensationalistic manner possible. Truth was sacrificed for blood-curdling entertainment. He even went so far as to create a dialogue that never took place as he "reported" testimony supposedly spoken by Ed. According to Johnstone's story, Ed testified in a lengthy rambling discourse how they had met the Colemans and shot their way out of a self-defense situation.

In the next edition the editor of the *Pepin Courier*, W.H. Huntington, took Johnstone and the *Pioneer Press* to task over the fabrications. While the *Press* was a daily newspaper, the *Courier* was published only once a week. In the November 25th edition the *Courier* gave its account of the events of the 19th when Maxwell was lynched. The story was written by an eyewitness who actually had been present in the courtroom and privy to the events downstairs and out on the front lawn.

In the same edition the *Courier* also chastised the reporter from the *Pioneer Press:*

> E.R. Johnstone ... evidently went away too soon as the lynching took place about two hours after he left town... we don't see the use of him coming at all. His report of the affair, written in St. Paul, but as if he had been an eye witness of the whole affair "lays over" anything of the kind we ever heard of.

The Durand editor made it plain from the outset that Johnstone was not in Durand when the lynching occurred. That point seemed verified by the editor of *The News* published in Menonomie. Rather than reproduce the Johnstone version, he chose to reprint the *Courier* story instead of "wild and conflicting" tales that the *Press* had issued. Huntington of the *Courier* remained blunt:

> His (Johnstone's) article is written in as sensational a style as possible and with as little truth as could possibly be worked in. He publishes a confession made by Ed in the court room, when in fact the murderer made no remarks at all, except to give his name, plead not guilty and say that he wished to waive examination.
>
> He tells of the red and blue shirted lumbermen who did the lynching, when in fact no such persons were in the town... But it is useless to mention all his lies — we simply deny the whole article, and express our surprise that so enterprising a paper as *The Pioneer Press* should tolerate such an unmitigated damned liar.

It was bad enough that Johnstone managed to pull a fast one by having his sensational piece of fiction printed in a credible newspaper. The real problem though was that the *Pioneer Press* apparently never printed a retraction or acknowledgement of the misleading facts. Smaller market newspapers and weeklies that had come to rely on the *Press'* reputation for honesty and sound journalism were left thinking that the story, as Johnstone recorded and the *Pioneer Press* published, was true. They in turn reprinted Johnstone's version almost verbatim.

A good example can be found in the *Macomb Journal* of November 24th, 1881. Johnstone's description of the crowd in the Durand courtroom portrayed men who "growl like wild beasts" and women who "shrieked" during some kind of "melee" in the court-room. According to Johnstone, Maxwell was grabbed from the stand while giving testimony and dragged through the court and down the stairs. All this time the people were hollering things such as "Choke him", "Burn him", "Hang him." It probably helped to sell newspapers and may have lifted the *Pioneer Press'* re-print stats for the month, but it conflicted heavily with the eye-witness accounts of the reporters who really were present.

The *Courier* claimed something much different about the incident:

> A regular legal execution could not have been conducted more quietly and orderly, and as soon as the murderer was suspended from the tree the crowd commenced to disperse. Less than fifty of the large assemblage in the courtroom had time to get out of the building before the tragedy was over. Five minutes after the body was cut down less than a dozen persons were to be seen about courthouse square, and our streets had assumed their regular every-day appearance. All seemed to feel that a painful duty had been performed, and expressed fervent wishes that the like necessity should never occur again.

The *Courier* accused the St. Paul journalist of trying to create a news story. It said that the "bull-headed reporter" was "expecting to see a lynching immediately on his arrival" and when nothing along that line appeared to be in the wind, that he "did all the talking he could to excite the citizens to take the law in their own hands." The *Courier* editor would certainly not be accused of being timid. Huntington brashly accused Johnstone of spending time in the local saloons "trying to stir up a mob". As far as the *Courier* was concerned,

Johnstone wanted to generate events for a story so that he could "get all the glory of writing it up for his newspaper."

"Glory" might not have been an inappropriately chosen word under the circumstances. The reporter, Johnstone, made a couple of efforts in the article which he produced to direct attention to himself. Reporters are supposed to be impartial, objective, to look at the action, not to infuse themselves into it. But Johnstone wrote himself into the script as a character in the unfolding drama. Of all the people surrounding Maxwell in his final days, according to the *Pioneer Press* writer, "This morning between 9 and 10 o'clock he sent for your correspondent…".

It seems, according to Johnstone at least, that Ed required some legal advice and apparently thought the best source might be from the young journalist whom he had only recently and briefly met:

> He took your correspondent into a corner and said, "I haven't any friends here … and I would like to ask you what you think about my waiving an examination. … I guess if I waive a hearing he (District Attorney) won't have much to get ready. What do you think about it? I told him I suppose a lengthy a prolonged hearing could do him no good and he then said: "I've made up my mind then, but I'll make a statement about the murder before I leave the court room."

From the account written by another journalist who really was present during Ed's appearance in the courtroom, we know that Maxwell at no time addressed the court regarding the events in Durand that fateful July evening. A great deal of suspicion was cast upon the accuracy of the claim by "your correspondent" regarding Ed requesting his advice. The suggestion didn't seem logical. Why would Ed seek legal advice from a young newspaper reporter? It wasn't as though they were close friends. They hardly knew each other. Johnstone goes so far as to say that during a conversation he had with Maxwell that Ed "… looked me straight in the eyes as he always does when talking … (and rested) … the irons on my breast." Warm and touching, but barely believable!

It might seem that the *Pioneer Press* was duped by one of its own reporters and was victimized from within, but that may not have been the case. The *Pepin Courier* wrote that its own staff had furnished the *Pioneer Press* with the "truthful and full account of the lynching, sent by special messenger to Menonomie before the body was cut down ..." The accurate description was telegraphed to St. Paul within less than three hours of the event, leading the editor of the *Courier* to wonder why the *Pioneer Press* suppressed that story and printed the one by Johnstone.

Courtesy Pepin County Historical Society

This photo is thought to have been taken a few years after the hanging of Ed Maxwell. He was hung from the tree at the left. The jail beside the courthouse was built after the lynching.

E.D. Dudley, of La Crosse, was in Durand the day of the lynching and was another eye-witness. He was only a spectator to the drama, not a reporter. He sent the *Chronicle* a full "and truthful account, from which we (the *Courier*) extract the following:

> The town was without unusual excitement. The court room was densely crowded, perhaps one-half women and children. Not twelve men in that building, perhaps, knew what was coming. The fact that all the citizens brought their families, as a rule; the fact

that the *Pioneer Press* reporter had left town, not three hours previous, having failed to scent anything in the air, shows that what was done was quietly planned. After the hearing and the commitment, as the crowd came down stairs into the hall below, a few men might have been noticed standing idly in the hall and on the platform. As the officers in charge of the prisoner reached the landing some one shouted "Hang him!" which was the signal for seizing the five officers instantly by two men, to each officer, and notwithstanding a terrible resistance, the suddenness and complete surprise of the attack was sufficient, and in less than three minutes from the time the prisoner started from the court room, he was hanging from the tree in the court house yard. It was the coolest performance I ever saw, and I doubt whether in the whole northwest there ever has been its equal for perfection of plan and execution; no notice, no hurrahing-. Not the least sign of a mob or mob elements – and before the hall was emptied, all concerned in the execution of justice were away or standing as quiet spectators. Within thirty minutes after all was quiet, no one in or around the buildings, or grounds and the town was as quiet as though no unusual thing had happened. There are none but what are satisfied and the best people here say, "This is our way, now and for the future; all who have any reason to fear this must stay away from us."

Dudley's letter-to-the-editor re-printed in the *Pepin Courier* served to reinforce the account written by its journalist. What makes Dudley's letter so valuable is not just the fact that it solidly verifies the *Courier's* rendition, but that the letter was unsolicited and not written for any gain.

Fortunately for the *Courier* editor, he didn't have to take on the large market newspaper by himself. The *St. Paul Globe* jumped into the skirmish of the ink by criticizing the *Pioneer Press*. Calling Johnstone's article "the most shameful deception ever practiced upon the public in this region ...", the editorial ridiculed the piece saying the author "... drew entirely upon his imagination." The following salvo fired by the *Globe* must surely have hit home:

...what does the public think of the fiction which the disreputable *P.P.* palmed off on its readers. The disgraceful feature is that a newspaper should have no regard for the truth in matter of news, but invent an entire report of such an affair and palm it off as genuine.... When a paper is so lost to decency as to willfully publish bogus news, nothing it contains from advertisements to market reports can be relied upon.

Since the *St. Paul Pioneer Press* today is a widely-read, well respected newspaper, maybe there were some valuable lessons learned from the *Globe's* condemnation of "bogus" reporting, leading it to mend its ways.

Even today researchers of the Maxwell saga are forced to discriminate among the versions from the past. Because so many newspapers picked up the service from the large market *Pioneer Press* and re-printed that account as the truth, there are far more misleading renditions than accurate ones to sift through.

Historical inaccuracy was not limited to the lynching story or to the *Pioneer Press.* There were several differing accounts of Kilian's capture of Ed in Nebraska and at least three different stories about Ed's escape from the Macomb jail. Similar multi-versions of the shooting of Sheriff Lammy exist also. Since the only "wire service" available in the early 1880's was the telegraph, it was understandable why confusions abounded when incidents occurred hundreds of miles away. Varying details resulting from word of mouth recounting were expected. But those were honest errors, not deliberately jaded accounts. There can be little compassion for reporters who would intentionally mislead for the sake of sensationalizing a story by complete fabrication. Johnstone re-wrote history before it became the past.

The DURAND JAIL

As TRAGIC AS THE murders were, they brought to light a problem that Pepin County was experiencing with its jail. As one reporter claimed prior to Ed's return to Durand, "If the Maxwells were housed here, they wouldn't stay long. Our jail wouldn't hold a vagrant."

While E.R. Johnstone, the *Pioneer Press* fiction writer, didn't always get his facts correct, he may have written his most truthful statement when he described the Durand jail:

> The jail, a common two-story frame house with iron gratings at the window and wooden ones inside – a flimsy, insecure structure throughout, stands on a little eminence about a block and a half from the courthouse and the latter is surrounded by a large yard in which are several small and one large tree, one with a projecting limb reaching to the walls of the building.

Johnstone had taken notice of the poor security that the jail offered. He had probably wondered how a facility such as that was expected to hold the likes of Ed Maxwell.

A newer jail built later solved another problem not mentioned in the report. Because the jail was a block and a half uphill from the court-house, prisoners would have to be transported that distance for their appearances, or they would be escorted on foot. The new jail was constructed beside the court-house, thus facilitating the movement of prisoners to appear before the bench.

Courtesy Dunn County Historical Society

The Pepin County Jail and sheriff's residence are on the left. Th‹ smaller section is the jail. In it Ed Williams was placed while waitin‹ to be taken to the Courthouse. Photo by Lawrence Cronk.

The date of this photo of the jail and courthouse is not given but it had to have been after 1895. Notice that the caption refers to the alias "Williams" rather than the correct surname of "Maxwell". However, the caption is wrong about this jail housing Ed. This jail was built next to the court-house after Ed was lynched. The date on the front section reads 1895.

The "insecure" conditions of the jail had been a source of contention for the Pepin authorities for some time. They were well aware of the failings of the structure. Only a year and a half earlier, the *Pepin Courier* had run an article outlining a report on the facility. Not used all that often, it said that only one prisoner was usually housed there about a quarter of the time. But it also mentioned that the last one (up to March 5, 1880) had torn up the floor and escaped through a hole in the wall.

A building in which a prisoner could literally claw his way out would definitely not hold for long the likes of the Maxwell boys. After bluntly stating that the jail needed to be re-built, the report detailed many of the problems:

The windows are so low that a person can communicate with the inmates, or can pass anything through the windows ... a single room; four cells; dark and damp... It is no fit place for even a convict.... The partition does not rest on the floor ... It is built on damp ground, and there are not enough windows; those that are there are too low.

The structural problems were bad enough. Worse were the sanitary conditions which the report went on to describe:

> The privy vault is just outside the building; originally there was a tunnel or tube running inside the prisoners' apartment, which they were obliged to use as a privy; it would get clogged and stink the prisoners out. The arrangement has been abandoned, but the vault is there yet, and the stench is bad in the prisoners department.

As if all that weren't bad enough, the jail rested over a sink-hole. The report suggested moving it to a "dryer and better location." Evidently more attention was paid to the jail's condition in the years that followed because a new county jail was added to the grounds next to the court-house. No doubt the report described in the 1880 report was instrumental in nudging the county powers to create some important changes.

The writer of the report? None other than Miletus Knight. Who would be more concerned about escaping prisoners?

MAXWELL EDITORIALS

As was to be expected, the end of Ed Maxwell wasn't the end of the Ed Maxwell story. What followed was a raging battle of the editorial pages. The *Courier* found itself in the unenviable position of trying to defend the citizens of Durand while at the same time denouncing vigilante justice. But give the Pepin paper credit; it did publish comments from the other newspapers that came out a little stronger against what had happened on the courthouse lawn.

Most newspapers condemned the actions. The *Madison State Journal* took a moral tone about mob rule. "...such things as lynchings ought to be prevented ... We must not override law and order, however great the grievance."

Not all the criticism was leveled at the mob members. Much of it was laid at the feet of the lawmen who were expected to protect their prisoner until he had a fair and complete trial. Peck's *Sun* came just short of accusing the officers of complicity in their role that day: "They (officers) must have known that there was danger of lynching, and while they may have thought it served him right, they should have made a show of protection...the sheriffs should have made resistance enough to have got knocked down or there should have been an official black eye or something to show for it."

Not everybody was opposed to the treatment given Maxwell. The *Courier* re-printed this cryptic comment from the *Washington*

Critic: "Wisconsin, by the way, is ahead of the times. She has just indulged in a first class lynch." No doubt the Washington comment was inspired by the recent death of President Garfield at the hands of the assassin, Guiteau. Another publication suggested that perhaps Durand, Wisconsin might be a good place as a change of venue for Guiteau. In fact, the *Courier* itself on another page made this observation on December 2nd:

> More than half the papers that condemn the lynching of Ed. Maxwell suggest that Guiteau be sent to Durand. What for? His crime is no worse than Maxwell's. President Garfield was a greater but no better man and citizen than Charlie Coleman, and if lynching is correct in one case it certainly is in the other... Stop your sniveling over Maxwell or else dry up your suggestions concerning Guiteau.

A similar light-hearted attitude was adopted by the *Dubuque Herald* which suggested "... let all the thugs and murderers be sent to Durand ... The people of that vicinity have a peculiar way of their own for arranging preliminaries that is quite commendable in some cases..."

Of course, no one in the *Courier* office should have been surprised at the outcome of November 19th. Five months before, in the heat of the Coleman murders, the local publication had written:

> Our community has suffered and borne too much already and it needs but a trifle to stir the smoldering wrath into a flame that will find suitable victims in short order. Lynch law is *sometimes* justifiable. (italics are in the original)

Probably the most straight-forward wording on the topic came from the *Galesville Independent*:

> Word comes from Durand that Ed Maxwell, alias Ed Williams, one of the murderers of the Coleman brothers, was hung to the limb of a tree on Saturday last, as he passed from the court house,

after being fully identified in the trial. Such summary justice is
shocking, but to our mind, is preferable to a cool, legalized murder
by a state. It was blood for blood, by the hands of a large number
of friends of the two, noble young men. It is no compensation for
the loss, but it is just retribution to the desperado and a warning
to thieves and ruffians. There can be no element of noble heroism
in those who commit theft and then shoot down officers in the
discharge of their duty even in self-defense. They start with rob-
bing honest people, and end in bloody crime. The press should be
careful to condemn and not exalt these desperadoes.

The Wabasha *Herald* put another spin on the outcome entirely.
It condemned the hanging, sort of, but then pointed out that in Wisconsin capital punishment no longer existed. If the fear of being
lynched was all that deterred the likes of the Maxwells, well .... :

Ed Williams one of the murders of the Coleman brothers has ex-
piated his crimes by a violent and tragical (sic) death at the hands
of a mob. We do not justify mob violence, but so long as the
extreme punishment for such crimes as were committed by this
desperapo (sic) and his brother is nothing but imprisonment, with
the chances largely in favor of ultimate pardon or escape, just so
long may we expect to see the people take the law into their own
hands in case of any unusually atrocious murder.

Capital punishment was abolished in Wisconsin many years
ago, and since, that time, the fear of a rope over the branch of a
convenient tree has done more to deter ruffians from committing
murder than the massive walls and grated windows of the State
prison at Waupun. It is a bad state of affairs when even such a man
as Ed Williams can be taken from the officers of the law and hung
without the form of a trial. But in this case substantial justice has
been done, and while we regret that he could not have been tried,
convicted and hanged in accordance with due process of law, we
aren't much inclined to find fault.

One other piece of fallout from the *Pioneer Press* story about the hanging came about in their editorial space. The *Press* claimed that after the lynching a coroner's jury rendered the verdict that Ed Maxwell died "'by falling down the court house steps and breaking his neck. The kind hearted citizens carried his senseless body out of doors and hung it up on a tree in the hope that the fresh air might revive him." The editorial was picked up by other papers and re-printed as though the comments were truth. The *Milwaukee Republi-can* used the story referring to the "Williams tragedy" as a "farce".

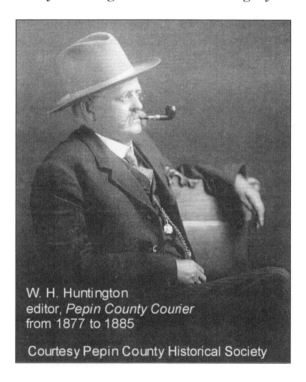

W. H. Huntington
editor, *Pepin County Courier*
from 1877 to 1885

Courtesy Pepin County Historical Society

Needless to say, the *Courier* editor responded in this war of words with both barrels blazing. Pointing out that there in fact was no coroner's inquest held at all, the Durand editor referred to the *Pioneer Press* story as a "sensational and lying report" and added that "the lie will travel further and faster than the contradictions..." But his sarcasm couldn't be missed with his parting shot: "We owed hu-manity a debt which was half paid by the lynching of Maxwell and if there are any more outstanding claims of this kind they will be settled on demand."

To be fair though, the *Pioneer Press* did run an excellent editorial addressing the punishment and offered an insight to its origin:

> The lynching of Ed Maxwell has its little moral too... The resort to mob violence ... is proof patent of a distrust, well or ill founded as it may be of the regular machinery provided by the State for the punishment of criminals... A community only takes the law into its own hands when it has lost confidence in the strong hand of the law.

The same editorial quoted in part here, while referencing the Maxwell hanging, was aimed also at the case of Guiteau, the assassin of President Garfield:

> (The general public) sees in the seemingly needless and gratuitous delays in the conviction of Guiteau only an attempt to place flimsy legal technicalities between a detested criminal and deserved punishment, and feels a strong impulse to brush them aside with the swift hand of private vengeance... It would be a rash assertion... that crime has steadily increased in Wisconsin since the abolition of the death penalty for murder ten or fifteen years ago... (however) lynching has become more common in Wisconsin than in any community east of the Missouri and north of the Ohio.

As the discussions heated up in the press, another interesting opinion about the events came from a surprising source. David Maxwell, Ed's father made the following comment published in the *Eau Claire News*, December 17, almost a month after the hanging:

> Lon and Ed were bad boys. I haven't a bit of a wish to defend them. They deserved punishment for their crimes, though I always shall believe they shot the Coleman boys in self-defense; but the same law they broke should have punished them, not a lot of cowards who feared to meet the lads when they were free.

Perhaps it's appropriate to leave the last words on the subject of retribution to none other than Ed Maxwell. Only a day before being dragged across the court-house lawn to the waiting oak, Ed, never bereft of an opinion, commented on Garfield's murderer:

> That was a cowardly act of Guiteau's and you bet I'd like to have a shot at him from my Winchester. I wouldn't miss him, you can feel sure of that, and I wouldn't wound him slightly either. Guess if I got away from here and killed Guiteau, the whole neighborhood wouldn't turn out and hunt me through the woods. Wouldn't you think?

The MYSTERY of ALONZO

THE BOY HE SENT into the store to buy some groceries had the last confirmed sighting of Alonzo Maxwell — ever!

Lon simply vanished. But his disappearance spawned many interesting stories and leads. In 1937 August Ender, who was then the publisher of the *Courier-Wedge* in Durand, wrote a lengthy article re-capping the saga of the Maxwell events. As part of his narrative, he offered two possible versions of Lon's disappearance which had come to his attention.

The first of the stories contained an almost heroic/ romantic bent to it. It went like this:

> After the Nebraska gunfight with Kilian and company, Lon headed out to Montana to begin a new life. Three years later in 1884, he was arrested in a wheat field near Miles City. It's not said exactly what he was arrested for, nor was any other information provided about the charges such as whether he was using another alias. He was subsequently sentenced to do time in Montana's State Prison at Deer Lodge.
>
> Loaded into a stagecoach for the trek across the prairie, he made a daring escape near Livingston by diving out the stagecoach window. Despite being handcuffed, the prisoner made a swift dash for freedom that seemed to be successful. Some versions of

this tale have him swimming across the Yellowstone River in his romp to the foothills in the mountain region.

Years later (some say one or two years), a skeleton was found in a mountain valley or canyon in the Livingston area with its wrists still bound in handcuffs. The assumption was that Lon died of starvation or disease.

Of course the story would be fitting; death while being punished for his crime; died like his brother still wearing irons; perished in a similar fashion to the way he lived – alone and independent, struggling to survive, but without his brother to aid him.

A good story all right, but without a written document anywhere to substantiate it. The court files in Miles City did not carry one word to verify that any such arrest was ever made. There were no records of any court proceedings having been carried out, nor any sentence given that resembled the described incident. In the Livingston area, there was not a reference in the newspapers (found by this author) outlining the discovery of a skeleton with or without handcuffs. No death certificate was issued there either that supported the claim. In short, with no official documents at either end, that plot might have been a fabrication in someone's imagination.

The second of the stories was somewhat more credible and again involved Montana. The details came from a credible source. Raymond Sheldon was a county attorney working on a case of land titling in Carter County in the southeast corner of that state about 1935. He was trying to do something known in legalese as "quiet a title" to a piece of land that had been homesteaded near Ekalaka.

According to a letter Sheldon wrote, "… Alonzo Williams filed on a homestead in Carter County under the name of William H. Spencer." This would not in itself seem outrageous. Hiding from the law for such serious crimes, it was only natural to expect that he would use an assumed name. Ed had once told a reporter that they often worked under false names, that one they used frequently was "Thompson", the name of Lon's in-laws. Thompson's first name was "William". Was Lon hiding partially under the guise of Fannie's step-father?

William Spencer had lived in the Ekalaka area for about 12 years. It was said that Spencer spoke very little about his past and was a "crack revolver shot". It seems that years before he and another neighbour came to blows over a lady in whom they shared a romantic interest. Spencer killed the other man with a club. He was arrested, but was acquitted in Miles City court on his plea of self-defense. Nothing further was learned about the lady.

About May of 1915 Spencer blew off the top of his head with a 30-30 rifle in a successful suicide. It was not a completely spontaneous notion because just prior to killing himself, Spencer asked a local boy to deliver a note to the boy's father, Earl Tooke. The note read "Friend Earl: Get word to Doc as soon as you can that I am a thing of the past. Come over and look after the stuff until someone gets here. Goodbye. W.H. Spencer."

Tooke rode immediately the half mile to the ranch where Spencer lived. He was too late to dissuade Spencer. The deed was complete. The man was laying on the floor with his rifle across his chest still pointing at his head.

No next of kin were located. A year previous he had made out his will naming the local physician, Dr. Colvin, his beneficiary, apparently to repay a financial obligation. No motive was ascertained save the fact that recently he had been "unsuccessful in business ventures" according to the *Ekalaka Eagle* that reported his death in its April 30th issue in 1915. The same article did say that "Bill" had been a "likeable character and had many staunch friends".

There was at least some truth to this story. William H. Spencer did exist in Ekalaka. He was buried in the Ekalaka Oddfellows Cemetery (now Beaverlodge Cemetery). His plot has a small groundmarker. No heirs were ever located despite the best efforts of the Carter County legal minds. The records were finally put to bed in January, 1946 since by that time the county had taken back the land for back taxes owing (probate # 418). The land was later sold by the county.

No records exist in either Miles City or Ekalaka showing a William Spencer on trial for murder or anything else. This might be a clerical or filing error. The county in which Ekalaka currently is located did not exist at the time of Spencer's residency there. It was still part of Custer County up until Carter County was formed in the years after Spencer's death. This fact is important because all official records to that time were filed at the county seat in Miles City, including the court records and death registrations. But the old records in Miles City did not reveal any suggestion of Spencer's court appearance.

The "S" is covered over by the piece under the nail but the faint outline of the raised letter can be discerned. Photo: L. Kruger

The suicide left his land title in an imperfect state and the county had to tidy up the affair of back taxes. That brought in Attorney Sheldon to examine things.

Sheldon admitted that there was little proof that Spencer was really Alonzo Maxwell. Something that at first seemed out of character was that Spencer had served in the 21st U.S. Infantry. But if Lon was looking for a place to hide where he would be anonymous, what better place to do it than in the army? By enlisting under an alias, he would eventually leave with an "official" status attached to his new name. The period of Spencer's enlistment appears to have been after the Spanish-American War. It goes without saying that, as Attorney Sheldon discovered, everything is conjecture and proving it now would be virtually impossible. Short of an exhumation and DNA testing, the secret will likely remained buried. Even a quick count of toe bones would be helpful.

With no concrete evidence of Lon's activities after the Nebraska gunfight, those intrigued by his story can only surmise how it might have ended. With his affinity for finding trouble, it's likely that he found himself at odds with the law again somewhere else. On the other hand, he did try once before to make a respectable new life for himself under an assumed name. Did he eventually sneak back to Osco to secretly meet again his parents and siblings? None of the answers would be easy to determine. For now, Lon has been simply lost in the graying mists of history.

THEIR FINAL CHAPTERS

Edward Maxwell:

Being lynched and buried in the Potter's Field at Durand Cemetery was not the finale for Ed. Some years later, so the story goes, he was exhumed and the skeleton given to a doctor in California for study. There is no verification for this story.

Although his was an unmarked grave, during that time-frame it was no secret where he was planted. The October 20th issue of *The Pepin County Courier* of 1882 carried an item stating someone had placed the Soldier's Monument from the cemetery "down near Ed Maxwell's grave". The article was titled "A Dastardly Outrage" reflecting the community's sentiment of the deed.

Over time, it seems, the Durand populace forgot Ed's exact resting place. In 1987 a study was done on the area south of Highway 10 to determine whether any bodies lay in a section of Forest Cemetery that might be part of Potter's Field. It seems that Highway 10 had bisected the cemetery years before and that there was a possibility of some graves being neglected on the other side of the road. A team of State Historical Society archeologists determined that had been the case. Among several ancient graves, one intact skeleton in a coffin was discovered to have a broken right thigh bone. This left folks to wonder if it were Ed Maxwell who had a rough trip down the court-house stairs on his way to the hanging tree. No doubt Ed would have reveled in the media attention this caused more than a hundred years later.

David D. Maxwell:

Ed and Lon's father is buried in the Osco Cemetery in Kearney County, Nebraska. Osco, only a postal station rather than a town, is no longer shown on maps. Unfortunately his tombstone has fallen over and lays flat. That of his wife, Susan, leans at an awkward angle beside his. They rest between two sons, Gilbert, who died in 1915 and James who died at age seven, two years before his older brothers shot their way into criminal history.

John Lammy:

Lammy remains to this day the only law officer killed in Calhoun County. His murder came eleven weeks to the day after those of the Coleman brothers. As a result of the research for this book, he was recently remembered as a Fallen Officer in Illinois and he was inducted on the national memorial in Washington in May of 2007.

John Churchman:

(member of Lammy's posse shot by the Maxwells at Fox Creek)

John died at his home in Kampsville, Illinois on March 19, 1890 of consumption. He had been a longtime friend of John Lammy. He had enlisted in the Union army during the War Between the States and it was believed that during his four years of service he contracted the disease that killed him. Like Lammy, he was very active in his community and rose to become a prominent figure. During his lifetime he held several public positions. He also amassed a certain personal wealth as a result of his good business sense. On his passing at age 45, the local newspaper reported that his was the largest funeral cortege ever assembled in Calhoun County. He is buried in Summit Grove Cemetery near Kampsville.

Frank McNabb:

(the other deputy sheriff in Lammy's posse shot in the shoulder by one of the Maxwells)

Frank died at his home on November 27, 1933 at the age of 75. If you're doing the math, he was 23 years old at the time of the shooting.

Miletus Knight:

A colourful and prominent figure in Pepin County's history, Miletus remained either sheriff or deputy from 1881 to 1892. Because he possessed such a large personal library, he was asked to write the History of Pepin County in 1892 which was published in the *Atlas of Wisconsin*. A businessman in Durand for many years, he made his living selling agricultural implements.

Sheriff Joseph Kilian:

Whether or not it was because he spent too much time in Wisconsin with the Maxwell incident just when the election for sheriff was being run back in Nebraska, Sheriff Kilian lost the November 1881 bid for the Hall County sheriff's office. He had been sheriff of Hall County since 1876. He was defeated by Henry C. Denman by a vote of 862 to 732. To keep food on the table for his wife and five children, "good-natured Joe" as the Grand Island Times called him, took a job working in H.H. Glover's store. He did not give up law enforcement. In 1889 he was recommended by the mayor to become the Chief of Police of Grand Island. However, the council did not confirm his appointment and the mayor withdrew his name. Kilian went into private business. In 1894 he moved his family from Grand Island to California where he died.

Milton Coleman:

Milt is still the only lawman killed on duty from Dunn County. Sadly his tombstone in Oakwood Cemetery in Menonomie is badly listing to one side. The lettering is faded, and despite the promise of the well-intentioned folks of a previous era, Milton does seem to be forgotten. At the entrance to Oakwood is a sign indicating where one can view the grave of the only soldier in the cemetery to have fought in the Revolutionary War, Stephen Tainter. Menonomie would do well to preserve in similar fashion one of its police heroes also.

Charles Coleman:

Charlie is the only law officer killed in the line of duty from Pepin County. Buried beside his parents, he was also interred in the same cemetery as the man who murdered him. His marker is not easily located and has been ravaged by a century and a quarter of weathering. For a man who died serving a town in the protection of its citizens, a little more detail could be provided in offering him the recognition he deserves.

It was generally believed that the Colemans were the first and second lawmen killed on duty in Wisconsin since becoming a state. Actually that unenviable distinction belongs to Sheriff Joseph H. Baker of Portage County, who in 1875 was also shot by a pair of brothers, Amos and Isaiah Courtwright. While attempting to serve an eviction notice and other court papers, Sheriff Baker was shot by one of the brothers who had fired from a second floor window. The sheriff was taken to a nearby house where he died the following day. The Courtwrights were captured and jailed. Less than a week later, an angry mob succeeded in its second attempt to lynch the two brothers. Both were buried in a single grave in the Plover Cemetery where Sheriff Baker is also buried.

John Doughty:

(helped Sarah locate Charlie after Perryville)

After returning to the 10th Wisconsin, Company "D" to which he and Charles Coleman had both belonged, he was taken prisoner after the Battle of Chattanooga on September 21, 1863. Of the rest of the company, only seven survived to fight after that battle. Whether John was released or escaped, a year later he was shot and killed at Danville, Virginia in another skirmish.

Sheriff Sever Severson:

Well-known and well-liked in the Menonomie area of Dunn County, Sever eventually went into business selling farm machinery for the McCormick Harvester Company. He was also engaged as a millwright, carpenter, blacksmith and wagon-maker. It was surprising that he had time left over to devote to his brief stint as sheriff. He died April 3, 1907 in the hospital at Eau Claire at the age of 73 after a brief illness.

William Kuhl:

Disenchanted with the Milwaukee authorities for being mistaken for Lon Maxwell and wrongly detained for weeks, Kuhl sued for personal damages. The wheels of justice often grind slowly, but eight years later Kuhl was awarded a settlement of $5, 319 in June of 1889.

Amy Beach:

Amy decided to keep the half-dollar coin given to her by Ed Maxwell an hour before the killing of John Lammy at Fox Creek. She was only nine years old at the time. Amy passed away many years later in her 80's, but as late as 1950 the coin was in the possession of her sister, a Mrs. Minnie Heavner.

Sheriff James O. Anderson:

Revered sufficiently by the people of Henderson County to serve as sheriff for a full decade from 1876 to 1886, Anderson went on to act as their Honorable Member to the House of Representatives for four out of five terms over the next ten years. Leaving the House in 1898, the next year he was appointed to a position as a Special Internal Revenue Officer in which service he remained until 1911. That same year he accepted the title of Superintendent of the Illinois Soldiers' and Sailors' Home at Quincy, Illinois where he remained for many years.

Charles C. Hays:

Charlie captured Ed & Lon at Beardstown while he had been a deputy. In 1876 he became Sheriff of McDonough County. Married twice, Charlie lived past the age of 80.

Captain Thomas Jefferson George and the Ludington Guard:

The Ludington Guard was described as a "spirited corps of young men" who had been organized into a cavalry unit. That changed a year after their manhunt for the Maxwell brothers. In November of 1882 the Guard was officially disbanded as a cavalry unit and was reorganized as an infantry. Thomas George had served several years as its leader. Later "Old Buckskin", as he came to be known, became the sheriff of Dunn County.

E.R. Johnstone:

Unorthodox journalism obviously didn't hurt Johnstone's newspaper career. By 1899 he had jumped ship from the *St. Paul Pioneer Press* to become the managing editor of the *Minneapolis Times.* In the interim, as a journalist, at least one writer considered him to be efficient enough to claim that by his individuality, he had "risen above the anonymity" of the bureau he served, that he was a young man "who would be conspicuous on a sinking ship or at a dinner table". Presumably his new role at the *Times* involved him more heavily in non-fiction.

Sheriff Josephus B. Venard:

Sheriff Venard served only one term in that position. It was long enough to put Ed and Lon in the Joliet Prison. Following his second year as the chief law officer, he again served Macomb in another role for about 15 years: that of Post-Master.

Margaret Coleman:
(Charles' wife)

Mrs. Coleman was pregnant with her eighth child at the time of Charles' brutal killing. When her son was born, she named him, Charles Milton Coleman to honour the two slain lawmen. Within the next four years, she met and married Gilbert Albert Hunt, residing with him at Bay Lake, Minnesota. It was a second marriage for both and each had children from their first marriages. They did not bear any children from their union. However, one of Mrs. Coleman's daughters eventually married her step-brother, one of Mr. Hunt's sons.

Sarah Jane Coleman Andrus:

The sister of Charlie who so faithfully sought her brother after the Battle of Perryville was married to Milton Andrus from Illinois. Less than five years into their marriage, Milton died in 1857. They had a daughter, Alice, named for Sarah's mother. Alice died in 1861 at the age of four. Sarah moved back home with her family following her husband's death. She never re-married. In later life she lived with a niece in South Dakota where she died at the age of 71 in 1914. As was her request, Sarah was laid to rest beside her husband and daughter in Adair, Illinois. In a curious twist of fate, she is buried barely ten miles from Macomb where Ed and Alonzo began their criminal careers that led to the death of her brothers.

Fannie Hussey:

(Alonzo's wife)

Her death and its direct consequence to this story are clear. But her Registration of Death does leave some murky water. Officially the cause of death is documented as "puirferal convulsions". Her name is given as Fanny (sic) Williams. That is most likely because at that point, Lon's true identity had not yet been established. The husband's name is Alonzo Williams on the registration. Her mother's name is recorded as Catherine Thompson rather than Bridget. No name is given for her father except to misspell his surname as "Hussy". (His name was William.) Fannie was buried in the Waubeek Cemetery next to her sister who had died in 1869 at the age of seven years.

Elder David Downer:

It's not clear what Downer's role was in the religious life of Lon (or Fannie). It was not he who married them. They were married by C.D. Field, a Justice of the Peace. Perhaps Downer simply knew Lon as part of the flock in the Hersey area. Downer too was no slouch with a rifle. His marksmanship was renowned. Many newspaper articles of that period commented on his ability. The *Hudson Star* of July 5, 1880 told how the pastor had given a shooting exhibit the previous day at the Independence Day celebrations in Hersey. Using a repeating rifle he broke 14 of 15 glass balls. He also put 15 shots into a six-inch circle and did it in eleven seconds. His rifle of choice was a Winchester rifle. On August 25, 1882 the *Pepin County Courier* claimed he could hit his targets with it as easily as other experts can hit the same with shotguns. It may have been a common enjoyment of marksmanship that drew Lon closer to Downer.

Flora Maxwell:

Ed and Lon's sister, Flora, eventually married John Lynn Hall and they had three daughters. She died May 2, 1932 in Webster County, Nebraska.

George Maxwell:

Ed and Lon were not the only Maxwells to be gifted with marksmanship abilities. Their younger brother, George, was an expert trap shooter, accomplishing this with only one arm. In 2006 he was inducted into the National Trapshooting Hall of Fame. On June 22, 2007, he was added to the Nebraska Hall of Fame. He is buried near Norman, Nebraska.

John C. Walker:

Certainly a bit player in this story, Walker was the man that Milton Coleman had gone to Wabasha the day he was killed to return to Menomonie. Walker was wanted to face charges of the robbery of Toft's jewelry store. For that heist, he was sentenced to two and a half years in prison. Released October 16th, 1883 (early for good behavior), Sheriff Miletus Knight picked him up at the prison gate to hold him for trial for two other robberies in Durand of Vantrot's Hardware store and Hoeser's shoe store. Apparently he was capable of good behavior only while behind bars.

It seems only fitting that mention be made of a couple of the landmarks in the story.

The Dorchester House:

In 1936 the home in front of which the Coleman brothers were shot was razed to allow for the intersection to Mondovi and Eau Claire to be widened.

The Hanging Tree:

The tree from which Ed Maxwell was hung appears in many old photos prior to the 1960's. In that decade it was removed to make room for new offices to be added adjacent to the court-house.

Courtesy Pepin County Historical Society

This photo, probably from the mid-1920's clearly shows what was no doubt the limb from which Ed Maxwell dangled on that chilly November afternoon outside the Durand courthouse.

Ed's Rifle and Ball & Chain:

These items (shown on pages 183 and 184) were taken from Ed by the law. After he was hung, the rifle, the ball & chain and the rope that hung him were kept for a number of years by the county. Some time afterwards, Pepin County raffled off the items. They were won by a man whose name has been forgotten over time. About 1935 Floyd Dudrey, who was undersheriff at the time, bought the items from the man. The rope was eventually lost in a fire. In 1991 Dudrey loaned the Winchester 76 and the ball & chain to the Pepin County Historical Society to be put on display for a time.

Alonzo Maxwell:

For the time being, Lon remains an enigma. His final chapter awaits another researcher, an historian, or a lucky individual who will somehow manage to uncover this last piece of the Maxwell puzzle.

On this topic it's only fitting that the last word goes to Sheriff Miletus Knight. Responding to the claim of yet another gaffe on the part of *The Pioneer Press* in June of 1883, Knight in his restrained sense of sarcasm wrote in the *Pepin Courier* "Any person producing the Lon Williams who has lost a second toe on the right foot can get the reward of $850 – but not a dollar for anyone having all of his toes."

Other DATES in U.S. HISTORY

James Gang robbed first train at Adair, Iowa July 21, 1873

Wild Bill Hickok murdered in #10 Saloon in Deadwood by Jack McCall Aug 2, 1876

General George Armstrong Custer dies at the Battle of the Little Bighorn June 25, 1876

James-Younger Gang tries to rob bank in Northfield Minnesota September 7, 1876

Crazy Horse surrenders. Soon after is murdered in custody September 1877

Chief Joseph surrenders ("I will fight no more forever.") 1877

Lincoln County War 1878

Sam Bass shot during a robbery at Round Rock, Texas. He died of his wounds July 21, 1878

Pat Garrett shot Billy the Kid July 13, 1881

Chief Sitting Bull was in the news for leading Sioux into Canada. He finally surrenders July 19, 1881.

President Garfield shot July 2nd, 1881

President Garfield dies September 19, 1881

Gunfight at the OK Corral (October 26, 1881)

Jesse James shot in the back by Robert Ford. April 3, 1882

Doc Holliday died November 8, 1887

Dalton Gang fails to rob banks in Coffeyville, Kansas October 5, 1892

ACKNOWLEDGEMENTS

THIS BOOK WOULD NOT have been possible without the kind assistance from a great many sources.

I had never before recognized the valuable work contributed to their communities by the various historical societies. Their contributions to this book were many and varied from supplying files on microfilm to coming up with just the right photos.

Special thanks to:

> *Frank Kennett* and the Dunn County Historical Society in Menomonie, Wisconsin
> *Terry Mesch* and the Pepin County Historical Society, Durand, Wisconsin
> *Grace Bartholet* for the invaluable assistance and continued support at the Minnesota Historical Society
> *Lewis Retzer* and the Calhoun County Historical Society, Hardin, Illinois
> *Maurice Lammy* of Kampsville, IL (great-grand-nephew of Sheriff John Lammy) for historical articles loaned to me

I must mention the work of *Vera and Richard Slabey* who did a great deal of transcribing of early documents that had been handwritten decades before. They saved me a great deal of time wading through the various writing styles. This is another example of the worthwhile efforts of historical society members.

Editing was done by *Nora Gould* of Consort, Alberta, Canada. A huge thank you goes to her for putting aside many hours to make sure my typos and writing were more accurate in the final version than the one she had to read. She is extremely thorough. Her generous support was very much appreciated.

BIBLIOGRAPHY

To AVOID MAKING THIS book look like a crossword puzzle with endless reference numbers, I have placed here most of the many sources from which I drew my research material. For the newspapers to which I referred, I included the dates where possible. Not all of the material was used for quoting, but did come in handy as reading reference material. In some cases the information for my sources was incomplete owing to the age of the documents.

One should take warning though, when approaching the newspaper articles. Very often they contradicted one another, or the details conflicted with what had already been established. It became necessary to cross-reference frequently or to read between the lines (or in the case of the *St. Paul Pioneer Press*, to consider the source).

I offer these resources in the hopes of assisting anyone else who becomes as engrossed in the Maxwell saga as I did.   LAK

The History of Henderson County by James W. Gordon, Munsell Publishing Company, Chicago, 1911.

Menonomie and Dunn County, Wisconsin: A Historical Sketch by Bella French

Knapp School: 100 Alumni Reunions 1898- 1998

Spring Brook Saga by P.M. O'Brien, Printing Professionals & Publishers, Florida, 1994.

They Died at Their Posts edited by Christine Granger Klatt, Dunn County Historical Society, Menonomie, Wisconsin, 1976.

Durand 1881 compiled by Vera Slabey, Pepin County Historical Society, Durand, Wisconsin, 1987.

Dunn County News (Menonomie, Wisconsin)
    May 28; July 16, 23, 30; August 6, 13, 20; October 1, 8, 22; November 12, 19, 26; December 3, 10, 17, 1881; April 21, 1910.

The Macomb Journal (Macomb, Illinois)
    July 22; August 12, 26; September 2; October 7, 1875; October 5, 12, 1876; March 22; June 28, 1877; March 10; June 23; July 14, 21; August 4, 11; November 17, 24; December 1, 1881.

Pepin County Courier (Durand, Wisconsin)
    March 5, 1880; June 17; July 15, 22, 29; August 5, 12, 19; November 4, 11, 18, 25; December 2, 9, 1881; March 3, 24, August 25, October 20, November 3, 1882; May 25, June 15, August 3, 17, 25, 31, October 19, 1883; January 7, 1936; June 18, 1987.

Stillwater Messenger (Stillwater, Minnesota)
    July 16, 1881.

The Calhoun Herald (Hardin, Illinois)
    May 13, 1886; April 15; May 6, 1982.

Griggsville Independent Press (Griggsville, Illinois)
    October, 1881.

Daily Illinois State Register (Springfield, Illinois)
    October 4, 1881.

The Ekalaka Eagle (Ekalaka, Montana)
    April 30, May 14, 1915; June 25, 1948.

Quincy Daily Whig (Quincy, Illinois)
    September 30; October 5, 1881.

St, Paul Pioneer Press (St. Paul, Minnesota)
    September 29; October 26; November 4, 18, 20, 21, 23, 1881.

Eau Claire Daily Free Press (Eau Claire, Wisconsin)

July 11, 12, 14, 18;November 18, 21, 22, 23, 24, 1881.

Kearney County Bee (Minden, Nebraska)
November 18, 1881

Hudson Star & Times (Hudson, Wisconsin)
July 5, 1880; July 15, 22, 29; August 5, 1881.

Grand Island Times (Grand Island, Nebraska)
November 10, 17, 24; December 8, 1881.

The True Republican (Hudson, Wisconsin)
July 13, 20; August 3, 1881.

The Oquawka Spectator (Oquawka, Illinois)
October 6; December 1, 1881.

For added reading, I also mention Adrian Percy's book, *Twice Outlawed*, published by W.B. Conkey Company, Chicago, (about 1910). With little factual information, Percy wrote a romanticized novel loosely based on some information available at the time of his writing.